Christmas
1972

Great Baseball Pitchers

Using ten all-time "greats" as examples, Jim Brosnan provides the Little Leaguer—or any other reader—with a better understanding of the diverse qualities that can make a pitcher great. The players included are: Mathewson, Johnson, Hubbell, Paige, Dean, Maglie, Spahn, Feller, Ford, and Koufax.

Great Baseball Pitchers

by JIM BROSNAN

illustrated with photographs

RANDOM HOUSE

NEW YORK

This title was originally catalogued by the Library of Congress as follows:

Brosnan, Jim.
   Great baseball pitchers. New York, Random House
 ₁1965₁
     183 p. illus., ports. 22 cm. (Little league library, 3)

     1. Baseball—Biog.—Juvenile literature. ɪ. Title.

   GV865.A1B7   927.96357   65—10493

   Library of Congress   ₁65f14₁

Trade Ed.: ISBN: 0- 394-80183-0   Lib. Ed.: ISBN: 0-394-90183-5

Photograph credits: Brown Brothers, pages 12, 18, 28, 57, 62, 74, 90, 98, 124, 173; Culver Pictures, pages 24, 37, 44, 56, 95, 176, 177; European Picture Service, pages 21, 39, 166; New York Daily News, pages 53, 60, 110, 121, 135, 142, 143, 147, 157; United Press International, false title and title pages; 2, 9, 26, 34, 41, 72, 79, 83, 85, 102, 104, 106, 114, 118–119, 120, 129, 161, 164; Wide World Photos, pages 5, 48–49, 69, 86, 88, 117, 132, 138, 152.

COVER: Marvin E. Newman

Contents

Great Baseball Pitchers

CHAPTER 1

What Is a Pitcher?

The major league pitcher is a skilled craftsman. He has the most important job in baseball, for play doesn't begin until he throws the ball. Whatever happens after the pitch depends a great deal upon what the pitcher has decided to do with the ball. His technique combines physical and mental efforts, and the success of these efforts determines the results of play.

Pitching technique is an acquired skill. Major league pitchers are made, not born. The proper combination of physical ability and mental aptitude demands actual experience, on the mound. Pitchers are credited with originating the popular professional sentiment:

"You can learn something new in every big league ball game."

Great pitchers can, and they do.

Students of pitching technique can learn by watching all major league pitchers . . . good, bad, or average. Any man who makes his living on the mound in the major leagues has some basic tools of the pitching trade. Of all the baseball players in the world only two hundred can pitch for big league ball clubs in any one season. Each of them makes some mistakes, and every one of them learns from the mistakes of others.

Great pitchers come in different sizes, shapes, and colors. The exceptional pitcher need not be bigger, stronger, or better endowed with athletic instincts than other players. He need not be tall, although the greater leverage of height and reach can add speed to his fast ball. His vision does not have to be acute beyond 65 feet, for his catcher provides the only target he must see. He need not have exceptionally quick reflexes. But great pitchers often are good fielders, who help plug the hole in the middle of the infield.

A pitcher needs good physical coördination, more

A catcher—Yogi Berra—provides a pitcher's target.

so than a batter, but less than a shortstop. He must have a reasonably strong throwing arm, and he must also be able to throw the ball where he wants to. Control is essential—both pitch-control and self-control.

Above all he must be able to concentrate, to coördinate his mind and body, so that he can throw a certain pitch into a certain area over or around the plate. Every great pitcher can make his pitch do a job. The type of pitch—fast ball or breaking ball—is not so important as the thought behind it.

"Have an idea!" is what the catcher, the manager, and the pitching coach tell the man on a major league mound. Knowing which pitch to select, and where to throw it, is the major part of a great pitcher's technique. The courage to select the pitch, the control to throw it properly, and the confidence in its ultimate success are hallmarks of a superior pitcher. Courage, control, conceit are the basic tools of these craftsmen on the mound.

There have been many great pitchers; more are made every season. The question, "Who was the greatest?" starts a useless argument. The game of baseball has changed, and pitching styles have changed considerably in sixty years. (If baseball did not change, it would not be possible to "learn something new in every game," as pitchers do.) The great pitchers of any era are prominent and distinctive. In a sport where notable achievement is common the great pitchers are outstanding, bigger than the big leagues in which they play.

Statistics can be used to measure the performances of different pitchers. But statistics confuse where they should explain; they omit qualities which are basic to pitching technique.

All great pitchers win ball games. The desire to win is an overpowering force in their nature. In a sense they are born winners. How they adapt and adjust their talent in order to win is the story of pitching technique.

A pitcher's style is determined by his talent and his temperament. He may be big and fast, modest but stubborn, and look a bit like Walter Johnson. He can be short, throw curve balls, and have confidence in his own cunning. That is, he may be like Whitey Ford. He may have to rely on one outstanding pitch (Sal Maglie threw mostly curves). Or he may use a wide variety of pitches (Satchel Paige claimed to have ninety different types to choose from).

There is the "power" pitcher, who tries to blow batters down with the sheer force of speed. Then there is the "motion" pitcher. He whirls his body into action, kicks his front foot high, twitches his head, changes the angle of his delivery and the pace of his pitch, and tries constantly to fool the batter and upset his timing. There is also the classic "control" pitcher, who can hit a dime from 60 feet. He knows just what pitch each batter can't hit, and he throws such a pitch to just the right spot in or near the strike zone.

Style reflects a pitcher's personality. The self-centered, nobody-can-beat-me character wins with the certainty that comes from sheer conceit. The calculating curver exhibits absolute confidence in his choice of the proper pitches. The sensitive, super-talented pitcher battles for self-control and, when he wins it, batters can't beat him.

In the last half-century the development of pitching technique has been a constant process. It may have been easier to pitch in 1914 than in 1964, but the problems the pitcher faced were the same. At one time, offensive strategy was limited, and pitchers with outstanding control dominated the game. As power-hitters developed and rule changes were made to benefit batters, pitchers tended to become more careful. The great power pitcher could still match speed against strength, but the pressure was greater. One mistake could cost him a ball game. Every pitcher was urged to add an extra type of pitch to his bag of tricks.

"The modern major league pitcher cannot get by with just two pitches," said Early Wynn, a 300-game winner. "He must have at least three pitches

Early Wynn, a 300-game winner.

and he should be able to change speed on his fast ball and one breaking ball."

A variety of pitches, an assortment of deliveries, a choice of pitching tools have always been the aim of a man seeking proper technique on the pitcher's mound. Controlling each pitch, each delivery, is much more difficult than learning the different ways of throwing a baseball. Patience and practice help make pitchers successful; great pitchers who can sustain their concentration and control over each of their pitches make pitching look easy.

Unorthodox or unusual pitches are rare. There is nothing new under the sun on the big league pitcher's mound. The human hand can grip the baseball in a limited number of ways; the ball can be released from a limited number of angles. Imagination and creativity are stymied by the facts of a pitcher's life. He still must throw the ball 60 feet and 6 inches, through a strike zone that varies only slightly with the height of various batters. From the mound even a big man's strike zone looks small, and every hitter can usually reach every point in the strike zone with his bat. While these facts may discourage faint hearts, great pitchers relish the challenge. A pitcher's problems have always been the same. Concentration and control are his answer to most of them.

If pitching technique is more complicated today than ever before, batters are to blame. The *average* batter of the 1960s is better, bigger, and more dangerous than the *average* batter of forty years ago. (The *exceptional* batters, the great hitters of any era, would do well no matter when they swung.) Home runs destroy a well-pitched game, and sixty percent of the players on any big league team can and do hit home runs regularly.

The great pitcher of today is a careful craftsman. Courage, control, and conceit are increasingly important to successful technique. The significant rise in the number of well-pitched games is a tribute to better coaching and to the way big league players respond to its challenge.

Great pitchers are better than ever.

CHAPTER 2

Christopher Mathewson

"BIG SIX"

(1880–1925)

Early in the century no athlete was admired as much as a major league baseball pitcher. Baseball was then recognized by all Americans as the National Pastime. It was beyond a doubt the most popular professional sport, and the pitcher dominated the game.

The standout pitcher of the time was Christy Mathewson. There had been other great pitchers—Amos Rusie, Cy Young among them—but Mathewson was the king. The idol of schoolboys and adult fans alike, Mathewson was a super-hero. His biographers compared him with the great political figures in American history. One writer said:

"Christy Mathewson was to baseball what Washington and Lincoln were to American government."

The importance of the game of baseball has not been so exaggerated since those days, but no man could have represented the best qualities of his profession as well as Christopher "Christy" Mathewson.

He was tall, blond, and handsome; smart, sincerely modest, and absolutely confident of himself and his ability. On the pitcher's mound he displayed flawless form and the basic fundamentals of pitching technique. He had a good fast ball and two types of curves, one of which broke in and down, the other out and away. He not only could throw the ball exactly where he wanted it to go; he also knew just when to throw it to a specific spot.

Mathewson was bigger and stronger than the average man on the mound. He was also able and willing to work more often than most pitchers. Even so he seldom turned out a less than creditable performance in a game. He was fortunate to play for a good ball club throughout most of his career. During the 16 years he pitched for the New York Giants under the first of the great managers, John McGraw, the team won five National League pennants and one World's Championship. And they were contenders for the flag nearly every year. In all, Mathewson won 373 games in the National League, a record that has never been bettered. Grover Cleveland Alexander also won 373 games in the National League, but he pitched three more seasons than Mathewson.

The great sports writer, Grantland Rice, was often asked to analyze and compare the many great pitchers he had seen in baseball. He made a convincing argument that Mathewson was the best of them all.

"Others had as great an arm, as much nerve," said Rice. "There were a few pitchers just as smart. But nobody had all those things at the same time except Mathewson. Besides, he had class."

The sports writers of Mathewson's day were as impressed with Christy's character as they were with his pitching. Mathewson won a large number of ball games every season, and he did it year after year. But in his day pitchers were expected to win a lot of games; there were other big winners in the early 1900s. Baseball players in general were rough and rowdy then, and McGraw's Giants were as wild and woolly a band of men as any. The New York sports writers who followed them on the road and covered their exploits were looked

Christy Mathewson (left) and John McGraw (center) pose with a teammate during their early days with the Giants.

upon as war correspondents.

Mathewson did not care for brawling, fighting, and carousing. He was a college graduate in a day when few ballplayers were even literate. He would just as soon talk quietly in a hotel lobby as yell loudly in the corner saloon. He saved his competitive energy for the ball field, and the difference between him and his teammates was considered both notable and admirable.

The New York press respected the admirable qualities of Mathewson's character as well as the excellence of his pitching technique. He became the Sir Galahad of his time, a fact that may have influenced the opinion of many fans. But even the professionals praised him. John McGraw, Connie Mack, and Babe Ruth were among the great baseball personalities who considered Mathewson the epitome of the Golden Era of Pitching.

Mathewson was big, strong, with an assortment of great pitches. He may not have been as fast as Walter Johnson, but neither was anybody else. He did not have the great curve ball of Alexander, but his was good enough. No pitcher has ever had better control of his pitches. Mathewson could make a ball curve either way, in or out, to any batter. His famous "fadeaway" was really a fast screwball, unique for its day. It was the "extra stuff" that helped make him an extraordinary pitcher.

Grantland Rice summed up Mathewson's style by saying:

"Matty was an ideal pitcher. He had brains, heart, and control. He rarely threw a pitch that the batter liked to hit."

The famous umpire, Bill Dinneen, saw Mathewson from even closer up.

"Matty knew every batter's weakness. He knew how to feed it, just where to throw the ball. He knew when to gamble, when not. He paced himself in easy games, but he always had something in reserve."

Mathewson's style was a batter's despair. As Johnny Evers, the second baseman with the Chicago Cubs, complained:

"All you got to hit at was the pitch Matty knew you couldn't hit. He could throw a baseball into a teacup from 60 feet away!"

Absolute control is a feature of any great pitcher's technique. It comes only with practice. Mathewson started pitching baseball at the age of ten, and by the time he was twelve he could throw both an in-curve and an out-curve. Much bigger than the average teenager, he had both the patience and the determination to make his arm and body do what his brain told him they must do in order to win, no matter what the competition.

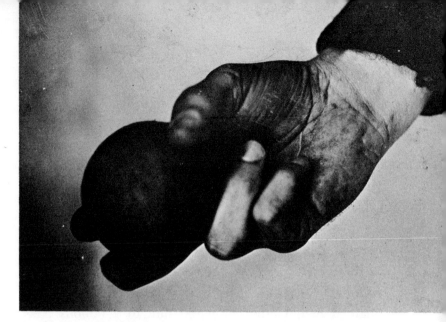

A close-up of Christy Mathewson's hand just before the delivery of his famous "fadeaway." He is holding the ball across the seams.

Professional baseball appealed to him because it offered the best sporting contest available. After leaving Bucknell College, where he had been class president, Mathewson joined the New York Giants in 1900. But he finished the season with Norfolk, of the Virginia League. Cincinnati then drafted him but, before he had pitched a ball, they traded him back to the Giants. Mathewson won twenty games for the New York team and thought he had established himself as a big league pitcher. But to his amazement he was told the next spring to play first base. The Giant manager, Horace Fogel, thought that Matty should play every day instead of pitching every third day.

John McGraw, who soon replaced Fogel, disagreed.

"Here's a kid with as fine a pitching motion as I ever saw and as much stuff as anybody. He'll pitch from now on."

For the next twelve years Mathewson did pitch, and he won twenty games or more in each of those years.

Mathewson was so impressively consistent, so dependable on the mound that a New York writer named Sam Crane compared him to a famous New York fire company with a reputation for being able to handle any emergency. Matty was able to quell any disturbance, douse any fire that National League batters started. When trouble threatened, McGraw called on Mathewson and "Big Six," as he was often called, took care of it. In three years he won over ninety games as the Giants drove to the World's Championship in 1905.

On October 9, 1905, McGraw led the New York club onto the ball field in Philadelphia to play Connie Mack's American League champions, the Athletics. The Philadelphia team was favored to win, but if the Athletics' supporters had seen Matty pitch they might have had some doubts. Mathewson, with his smooth, slick motion, was never better as he shut out the Athletics, 3–0.

Three days later, again in Philadelphia, Matty blanked Connie Mack's dazzled sluggers a second time, with a score of 9–0. The baseball world had never seen anything like it.

On October 14, the score in games for the Series was 3–1, with the Giants in the lead. Each game had been decided by a shutout. Mathewson took the mound against Chief Bender, the Athletics' only winner so far. The New York ball park was jammed with more fans than had ever watched a baseball game before. Matty was untouchable. Although the Giants scored two runs, they needed only one. For the third time in less than a week, against the best competition in baseball, Mathewson pitched a shutout victory. In three games against the Athletics, he allowed just one man to get as far as third base. He walked one batter, struck out eighteen, and gave up only fourteen hits. Had he never pitched another baseball his fame would have been assured. It is unlikely that any pitcher will ever equal his performance in the 1905 World Series.

Mathewson's control was legendary. In 1908 he pitched 416 innings and walked only 42 batters. In 1913 he worked 68 consecutive innings without walking anybody. But he was not throwing the ball over the plate just to *avoid* a base on balls. His pitching was consistently powerful, and he could

strike out a batter when he had to. In all, he fanned 2,505 batters in his career. He knew that some of them simply couldn't handle certain pitches. When necessary, Matty threw just those pitches. Control made it possible.

At West Point one year he gave an exhibition of pinpoint accuracy to the cadets. An officer had bet that Mathewson wasn't as sharp as he claimed he had to be to achieve success. Matty accepted the challenge. He was asked to throw twenty pitches— including three curves—into a catcher's mitt propped up behind the plate. For Mathewson the assignment was simple. He had blown down batters under much more serious circumstances.

The custom of the day was for pitchers to get batters out as quickly as possible. Home runs were rarities, and at least two hits were generally needed to score a run—especially if the pitcher didn't walk anybody. Mathewson once pitched a four-teen-hit shutout! When he got himself into trouble he knew how to get out again.

With the bases empty Big Six simply pitched to the catcher, throwing strikes. In a run-scoring posi-tion he was a different pitcher. Knowing what the batter was likely to hit, Matty gave him something else to swing at. No one has ever figured out a better style of pitching.

All pitchers have bad days on the mound; most

Mathewson's pitching was consistently powerful.

Five Giants photographed during the 1915 season: (left to right) Fred Merkle, Larry Doyle, Christy Mathewson, John McGraw, and Fred Snodgrass. By this time it had become apparent that Mathewson was wearing himself out.

pitchers have one or more poor seasons in their careers. Mathewson was considered to have had a bad year in 1914. All he did was win 24 games! Unfortunately the Giants lost the pennant that season, so somebody had to be blamed. Mathewson revealed that he had had a sore arm most of the year, and during the next spring it became apparent that he was wearing himself out.

Halfway through the 1916 season, John McGraw
called the Cincinnati Reds and told them he would
like to make a trade.

"Mathewson can't pitch any longer but he would
like to be a manager. You can have him if you
like."

At the age of 36, Big Six was finished. He did
pitch one game for Cincinnati, a team that he had
beaten 64 times—22 times in a row. On Labor
Day in 1916 he won his 373rd victory, but he was
staggering by the end of the game. He knew he
was through pitching in the big leagues. When
Mathewson returned from serving in the army during World War I, he took a coaching job with the
New York Giants.

John McGraw had contempt for the brains of
most pitchers, and he seldom allowed them to
make any of their own decisions on the mound.
But McGraw had both fondness and respect for
Christy Mathewson.

"Matty always knew what he was doing," said
McGraw.

Christy Mathewson set the pattern for all the
great pitchers who would follow him in baseball.

CHAPTER **3**

Walter Perry Johnson

"THE BIG TRAIN"

(1887–1946)

Pitching is easy . . . if you are Walter Johnson or a reasonable facsimile.

But fortunately for the great batters of professional baseball there has been only one Walter Johnson. He is the man with the greatest pitching arm in baseball history. There may never be another pitcher like him.

Technically speaking Johnson was more of a "thrower" than a "pitcher." He used no tricks. He simply threw a fast ball. If that didn't work, he threw a faster one.

Batters who had to hit against him needed no scouting report on his pitches. Ty Cobb, who had the best batting average of any player of the time, said:

"You knew you were going to get a fast ball from Johnson. You could get set for it. But you *still* couldn't hit him!"

The average batter who faced Johnson could only follow the advice of a minor league player named Reedy, who said:

"When you see his arm go up, swing."

The chances of the bat's crossing the plate at the same time as Johnson's pitch were not very good. Johnson struck out more batters than any other pitcher in baseball history. A record number of 3,497 men fanned the breeze as Johnson's third strike zipped into his catcher's mitt.

Johnson could have struck out even more batters than he did. But by nature he was a kind man who didn't like to embarrass anyone, even batters who were trying to beat him in a ball game. His teammate, Clyde Milan, said of him:

"Walter liked young kids, guys just breaking into the big leagues. He'd lay the ball in there, and *let* them get a hit! In fact any time he had the lead in a game he'd give away base hits. Nobody should have hit his stuff! It used to make me mad when they did."

Carl Hubbell, the great Giant pitcher of the 1930s, saw Johnson when Walter was at the end of his career. Hubbell thought Johnson's pitching delivery was the finest motion ever developed. Smooth and effortless, Johnson's pitching motion appeared to be easy exercise, a sweeping sidearm action that looked simple from the sidelines. But batters had to see the ball to hit it, and Johnson's fast ball was just a blur when it reached the plate.

"I had to ease up on pitches to certain catchers," said Johnson. "Not every man could catch me. When I was pitching the ball high or low, it was murder on the catcher."

It was murder on batters, too. And even on umpires. Billy Evans was umpiring behind the plate in one game when Johnson came in to relieve. It was the seventeenth inning and the Washington Senators had their third-string catcher trying to hold Johnson's fast ball. One pitch sailed past the catcher's glove and nicked Evans on the ear as he tried to duck away.

"Next thing I did," said Evans, "was to announce: 'Game called on account of darkness!' The sun was still shining, but my life was worth more than a couple more innings of that game." Johnson took it in his stride, uncomplaining as always.

In Johnson's day baseballs were not changed very often during the game. The first pitch of the

Frank "Home Run" Baker of the Philadelphia Athletics.

game was made with a clean white baseball, but from then on the players used the same ball as long as it stayed in the ball park. Scuffed, dirty, cut up, the old-time baseball was easier to pitch because it was harder to see.

Knowing that his fast ball was difficult to follow, Johnson worried constantly that he might injure or even kill a batter with his pitches. The Washington trainer once needled him about the bench-jockeying of Frank ("Home Run") Baker, a Philadelphia Athletics star. Baker's remarks had angered Johnson's teammates, and had even gotten under the skin of the gentle Johnson. The Washington trainer told Johnson that, if he didn't knock Baker down with a pitch, he wouldn't think much of him.

So Johnson let one go high and inside. Baker dropped safely out of the way, but Johnson said later:

"I wished I had it back as soon as I threw it."

The fearless Cobb actually crowded the plate against Johnson, hoping he would let up a little on his pitch. But even Cobb's best efforts against "The Big Train" (as sports writer Grantland Rice called Johnson) were usually bunts.

Reminiscing in later life, Cobb admitted that he had had a few embarrassing baseball experiences, "especially in Washington on any dark afternoon with Walter Johnson pitching!"

In Johnson's time there were no night games, no lights to turn on as evening shadows crept toward the pitcher's mound. It was an era of low-score, extra-inning games.

"At dusk," Umpire Billy Evans once recalled, "players used to pray that the game would end before they had to bat against Johnson."

The Washington Senators owned Johnson's contract during his entire baseball career. He was often credited with keeping baseball in the nation's capital, for the Senator teams with which he pitched invariably finished in the second division. Although he won 416 games for Washington, Johnson had to wait seventeen years before he got into a World Series. By then he was a national hero. Baseball fans all over the country rooted for him to beat the New York Giants. When he lost the first game 4–3 in 12 innings, and was knocked out in the fifth game also, his chances seemed dim. But back he came in relief to win the seventh game, 4–3. At 37 he still had that great arm, that wonderful speed. His manager, Bucky Harris, thought it was not only fitting but necessary that the Big Train should pitch the final innings of the world's championship game.

Born in Kansas, reared in California, Walter P.

Johnson's sweeping sidearm action looked simple.

Johnson was pitching in Weiser, Idaho, when major league scouts discovered him. Arizona and New Mexico had not yet been admitted to the Union, and Idaho was truly bush league country. The Washington scout complained bitterly about having to tramp through the wilderness "just to see some palooka who's striking out a bunch of semi-pros."

One look at Johnson's fast ball, however, was all the scout needed to stir prophetic visions. Whipping out a hundred-dollar bill, he begged Johnson to head east to pitch in the big leagues. Johnson held out for a round-trip ticket, but he did sign a contract.

The Senators used him initially against Ty Cobb's Detroit Tigers. The players were unimpressed at first. He looked like any other great big kid with a slow windup and an easy motion. He didn't even snap his wrist at the end of his delivery in order to put a little extra stuff on his pitch. He didn't need it. His fast ball was not only terribly quick; the smooth deliberate motion also made him "sneaky" fast. After he had pitched his first game, the consensus was:

"In two years he'll be greater than Christy Mathewson."

Johnson eventually won more games, pitched more shutouts (113 during his career), and fanned more batters than Christy. Had he played for a

The famous pitching hand of one of the greatest twirlers of all time—Walter Johnson.

better hitting club, Johnson might have won as many games as Cy Young, who had 511 victories between 1890 and 1911. Young was still pitching for Boston when Johnson broke into the majors.

"He's fast," said Young when he saw Johnson pitch, "but he's not the fastest I ever saw. Amos Rusie was faster. And neither one was quite as fast as me."

Old-timers were always putting down the rookies in those days, too. Nobody measured the speed of fast balls then, but Johnson's were fast enough. Since he had no other pitches to work with, his records are astounding to professionals who analyze technique.

He pitched more shutouts than any man in baseball history, starting off well in 1908 with three
shutouts in four days against the New York Yankees.
The Yankees were not so powerful in those days,
but they were professionals, and as such they were
visually shocked by the great Johnson fast ball. A
pop fly was a moral victory for batters who could
scarcely be expected to hit what they could hardly
see.

Johnson was a modest man who didn't drink,
smoke, curse, or argue. But he was stubborn and
absolutely sure of himself on the mound. Knowing
what it took to win, he was perfectly serious when
he said after one game: "I didn't deserve that one.
I didn't have my usual stuff." Washington had
won the game, 2–1, and their total of two runs
was more than Johnson had expected to get.

He pitched in fifty-nine 1–0 ball games during
his career, a third of which he lost. But he seldom
complained. In one eleven-inning, 1–0 loss, his center fielder, Milan, let a ground ball go through his
legs for the error that led to the only run. Sports
writers who caught Johnson unlacing his shoes after
the game asked him how he felt about the tough
break.

"Well, now, Zeb doesn't do that very often, you
know," he said quietly and pulled off his spikes.

For twenty-one years Washington fans idolized

Johnson shakes hands with Billy Evans at a ceremony honoring "The Big Train's" 21st year with the Senators. Evans umpired Johnson's first game with the Senators.

Johnson. Washington ballplayers praised him, and Washington's general manager, Clark Griffith, loved him. His appearance on the mound was the key to whether the team made or lost money at the gate. Headline notices followed every announcement that he would pitch.

His teammates called him "Barney," after the racing driver, Barney Oldfield. Handling the wheel with his big right hand, Johnson drove a car in the same way he pitched. Of course his fast ball moved more rapidly than the old-time automobile.

There were a few hitters in his day who claimed that they could hit Johnson. Eddie Collins, an infielder now in Baseball's Hall of Fame, said:

"Walter had a habit of throwing his curve ball whenever he got two strikes on a batter. He didn't *have* a curve, just a wrinkle. So I'd take two strikes and look for that little curve."

When Johnson stuck to his fast ball, he was often untouchable. In 1912 he won 16 straight games in a period of 7 weeks; in 1913 he pitched a dozen shutouts, won 36 games, and was unscored on for 56 consecutive innings between April 10 and May 16. The latter record will probably stand for all time. His career ended just before the era of the long ball, the age of the powerful home-run hitters, when any man swinging a bat might hit the ball out of the ball park.

In 1927 Johnson caught the flu in Tampa, Florida, the Senators' spring training base. He won only five games in that final year, but the fame of his fast ball endured and left its mark. Even today players who compare the American League with the National League say:

"Over here the pitchers throw *hard*. The National is a curve-ball league!"

In 1946, when Johnson was dying from a brain

tumor, he was asked what he considered his greatest game. Clark Griffith, who was at Johnson's bedside, answered for him.

"It was a 15-inning game. Washington won, 1–0. Johnson beat Rommel and he never threw harder."

Johnson grinned in agreement. That was his kind of pitching.

CHAPTER **4**

Carl Owen Hubbell

"KING CARL"

(Born 1903)

According to the dictionary, "screwball" is a slang term for a person with odd or peculiar ideas. According to the professional baseball player a "screwball" is a pitch with odd or peculiar motion.

Carl Hubbell was a screwball pitcher. He threw baseballs with his left hand, and some persons consider any left-hander naturally odd or peculiar.

Hubbell, however, was a quiet, soft-spoken, serious man. He had firm convictions about the business of pitching, and that resolution was neither

Carl Hubbell's valuable left arm goes into action.

odd nor peculiar. It might well stand as a candidly positive, and at the same time simple, theory of the pitching art:

"A pitcher must control everything he throws. He must perfect the one pitch he wants the batter to hit. Then he must make the batter hit that pitch."

Hubbell's best pitch was unorthodox, hard to throw, hard to control, and hard to hit. The screwball is a reverse curve, a breaking pitch that has an opposite action to that of a normal curve ball. It is the same pitch that Mathewson called a "fadeaway."

Hubbell's screwball, thrown left-handed, broke into left-handed batters, but away from right-handed batters. Because timing and coördination are so im-

The celebrated Giant's best pitch was the screwball.

portant to hitting the ball, batters—who seldom see
a screwball—have a difficult time hitting it. Every
pitcher would like to develop such a pitch. Few
do.

As a minor league pitcher, Hubbell had trouble
getting right-handed batters out. During the early
1920s, there were no coaches to help struggling
young pitchers. Hubbell, however, formed a habit
of watching other pitchers, both on his club and
on other teams, to see how they worked on certain batters. As Carl himself put it:

"We more or less had to learn on our own. And
a player stayed in the minors until he was ready
for the big leagues! I learned from studying successful pitchers, learning what made them successful, and trying to apply myself the best I could."

Hubbell had noticed that one particular south-paw was very effective against right-handed bat-ters. "He had a good sinking pitch that he kept down and away from them. I started to develop the same thing and eventually came up with the screwball."

Hubbell's simple statement does not take into ac-count his determination to develop an outstanding, big league pitch, the long and patient practice that gave him control over it, or the excessive strain on his arm. His screwball demanded an unnatural twisting of his left wrist and forearm that eventu-ally distorted the shape of his whole arm. Before he finished his pitching career, Hubbell's left palm faced out rather than in. This odd and peculiar deformity was permanent and once caused Pepper Martin, the St. Louis Cardinal third baseman, to say:

"Look at that! No wonder Hubbell's so good. He's a freak!"

Although Hubbell's entire big league career was spent with the Giants, he originally belonged to the Detroit Tigers, who bought him in 1926 and took him to spring training. One of the Detroit coaches, in a moment of bad judgment, told him that he should stick to fast balls and curve balls. The screwball, he said, would ruin Hubbell's arm.

But Hubbell was only half a pitcher without his screwball, and the Tigers sold him to the Beaumont, Texas, club where he pitched until the middle of July, 1928. He was not quite 25 years old when the New York Giants bought him for $40,000.

Giant scout Dick Kinsella had seen Hubbell pitch a game against Houston in the Texas League. He was so impressed with the skinny left-hander that he immediately wired John McGraw, the Giant manager, and said that he had found the left-handed pitcher New York needed.

"Reminds me of Art Nehf," said Kinsella.

"That's good enough for me," said McGraw.

The Giants soon learned that Hubbell wanted to throw screwballs to right-handed batters. Shanty Hogan, the New York catcher, said:

"Good. You keep firing that thing and we'll go places."

McGraw scoffed at the notion that a pitcher with a screwball was bound to ruin his arm.

"Matty threw it all the time. It didn't hurt him."

Christy Mathewson had called his screwball a "fadeaway." It curved into right-handed batters and faded away from left-handed batters. Mathewson had been the greatest right-handed pitcher in Giant history; Hubbell was to become the best of their southpaws.

In 1929 Hubbell pitched a no-hit game against Pittsburgh. But it was under Bill Terry, who succeeded McGraw as Giant manager, that Hubbell blossomed. The New York press called him "The Meal Ticket," the one pitcher who could be depended upon to win.

In 1933 Hubbell had 23 victories, including 10 shutouts. Pitching an 18-inning, 1–0 win over St. Louis, he allowed just 6 hits, fanned 12 batters, and didn't give up a single base on balls. His control was amazing, especially for a left-handed screwball pitcher. Throughout his career he walked fewer than two batters per game and occasionally pitched an entire game without ever getting behind on a batter.

On July 13, 1933, he started a stretch of 46⅓ consecutive scoreless innings, still the all-time National League record. Pitching many of his games in New York's Polo Grounds, Hubbell had to contend with fences that were less than 300 feet from the plate. They invited cheap home runs. But Carl was careful. He would throw a fast ball a bit too high, his curve down low, and then come into the strike zone with the twisting screwball, perfectly controlled. Batters beat it into the ground and moaned all the way to first base and back to their dugout.

Success leads to fame, and fortune usually follows.

In 1933 Hubbell had 23 victories, including 10 shutouts.

Hubbell was well paid by the Giants, but he never argued about money. One spring he was offered a blank contract, and filled it out with a salary figure that the Giants thought was too low. They gave him a $2,000 raise and added their unqualified admiration for a modest and honest man.

Hubbell had a lanky, almost skinny body. His heavy black brows, big ears, and sunken cheeks gave him a gaunt, almost sad face. In an era of rowdy, boisterous ballplayers, he was oddly, peculiarly unexcitable. His pitching philosophy was simple and positive, and he was imperturbable in the face of poor support or bad luck.

"Nobody makes an error on purpose," he would say. "When it happens, everybody has to bear down harder to cover it up. When a pitcher lets mistakes bother him, he loses his concentration."

Hubbell, the craftsman, was convinced that control was mostly a matter of concentration. "I would keep a mental picture of the flight of the ball into the spot where I wanted to make my pitch. And I'd keep that picture right through my windup and until I delivered the ball."

The pitcher who controls himself controls the game. Since he couldn't control good or bad luck, Hubbell didn't allow thoughts of luck to disturb his plans.

"Anyway," he said, "luck changes. Some line

drives hit off you are caught and you win. Some fall in, you lose. So long as my arm felt good, and my screwball was working, I was all right."

During his sixteen years with the Giants, Hubbell won 253 games, pitched for three pennant winners, and one world championship. Still, he is best remembered for a single performance—three innings of classic pitching in the 1934 All-Star Game.

The American League stars included some of the finest batters of all time. All of them were sluggers, and most of them were at the peak of their careers. Babe Ruth, Lou Gehrig, Jimmy Foxx, Al Simmons, and Joe Cronin made up the heart of a powerful lineup.

Hubbell was chosen to start the game for the National League, so he and his catcher, Gabby Hartnett, went over the list of hitters in the dugout before the game.

"We decided they had seen lots of fast balls and curves but maybe not so many screwballs. So the best thing to do was to throw some fast balls and curves but not where they could reach them. Then we'd come over the plate with the screwball."

When the first two batters reached base, however, and Babe Ruth stepped in to hit, Hartnett called time and went to the mound.

"Look," he said to Hubbell, "just throw that

Babe Ruth

Jimmy Foxx

thing. We'll be all right."

Ruth could hit the ball out of sight, but he was not a fast runner. Hubbell figured that he could get a cinch double play if he made Ruth hit the ball on the ground. But Ruth didn't even take his bat off his shoulder as Hubbell fired three screwballs over the plate for strikes.

Lou Gehrig was next. And he, too, might have hit into a double play. That's what Hubbell wanted, but Gehrig couldn't hit the *thing.*

"Then," said Hubbell, "we went all out to fan Foxx."

Four more screwballs and King Carl had struck out the side.

In the second inning Hubbell was still going strong. Simmons fanned. So did Cronin. And Bill Dickey had two strikes on him before he singled. Hubbell's pitching had the fans in the stands cheering as Lefty Gomez, the American League pitcher, came up to hit.

"You are looking at a man who is hitting .104," said Gomez to Hartnett. "What am I doing up here?"

Hubbell struck him out. In three innings he threw 51 pitches, 27 of them strikes. Only 5 pitches were hit by the slugging American League lineup. But Hubbell shrugged off his incredible success.

"We did what we planned and it worked out well."

Hubbell insisted that an even temperament was the key to successful concentration. He studied batters constantly, had a very good memory, and was able to sustain his concentration throughout an entire game. In 1936 and 1937 he pitched the Giants to two pennants, winning 48 games, 24 of them in a row. No other pitcher had had such a string of successes during regular season competition, but Hubbell's record went unrecognized for he had won his last sixteen decisions in 1936, his first eight in 1937.

"That's all right," said Hubbell. "I lost a game in the '36 World Series and that busted the string right there."

By 1938 the screwball had twisted his arm out of its natural shape, and Hubbell's career began to decline.

"I couldn't snap the ball in the late innings any more," he said, shaking his head.

His control was still sharp, and he was always a better than average pitcher, but his reputation as The Meal Ticket faded away. With his bread-and-butter pitch gone, Hubbell had to serve up the kind of stuff batters liked to cut at.

Hubbell's fame was assured, however, and the Giants would never let him go. After he finished

his active career by winning four games in 1943, Hubbell took over the Giants' farm system to develop new players. He taught the power of positive pitching to young Giants.

Twenty years later he was still running that farm system, still looking for another Hubbell.

By 1938 the screwball had twisted Hubbell's arm out of shape; his pitching career began to decline.

CHAPTER 5

Le Roy Paige

"SATCHEL"

(Born 1906)

The tall, thin figure of Satchel Paige casts a long shadow over the pitching mounds of baseball history. For twenty years he was the greatest pitcher in South American, Puerto Rican, Santo Domingan, Cuban, and Negro American baseball. And, after Negro players finally broke into major league baseball, he was for one year (1952) the best relief pitcher in the American League. At that time he was 46 years old. His unusually long playing career made him the dominant pitcher of the century.

Paige's age was always a carefully contrived mystery. Satchel mixed the figures on his birth date the same way he mixed his many pitches. He wanted to keep inquisitive interviewers off balance. Even his mother pretended not to know the year he was born. (Actually he was born at Mobile, Alabama, on July 7, 1906.)

The Paige era spanned modern baseball. For 38 years, in more than 2,500 professional games, with a million tricky pitches Satchel bewildered batters of all sizes, races, abilities, and reputations.

Variety was his style; control was his weapon; surprise was his element. He had more ways to get the ball up to the plate than any man alive. His control was so sharp that he could hit a dime from 60 feet four times out of ten throws. Easy to catch, he was hard to hit.

Paige's fast ball looked to some batters "no bigger than buckshot." He admitted, somewhat immodestly, that he usually threw nothing but peas.

Yet he could be cute—a craftsman with slow curves, fast sliders, sinkers, knucklers. He also had a soft blooper that arced high and dropped over the plate and a hesitation pitch that was the logical extension of the ordinary change-of-pace. (The American League president, Will Harridge, declared the hesitation pitch illegal in 1948, although he had to write a new rule in order to ban it.

Paige never found it necessary to violate established pitching regulations.)

Satchel claimed that he didn't learn to throw a good, fast curve ball until he was 54 years old. He was pitching for Miami in the International League at the time. That gave him 90 pitches, give or take a couple, to use on any batter willing to swing against him.

He had a variety of fast balls—hummers, bee balls, jump balls, trouble balls, hurry-up balls. He developed trick pitches "to rest my arm and work out the tiredness." Satch threw Alley Ooops, screwballs, bat dodgers, an eephus ball, and a slider that "cracked like a whip," according to American League umpire Bill Summers.

Incredulous listeners to Paige's stories suggested that he renamed the same pitch four or five times just to confuse his audience, especially batters. But Paige insisted that his grip on the ball determined its irregular line of flight. His "bee ball" was thrown overhand with his fingers on the smooth hide of the ball. Throwing the ball with his fingers across the seams produced a "jump ball." Every time he let a ball go in a different way he created a new pitch.

He seldom used the same windup twice. At times he looked like a windmill twirling in a cyclone. Or else he would stand as motionless as a scarecrow waiting for the batter to tire, grow anxious, or tense. Then *pop!* He would fire a hummer past the off-balance hitter.

Paige had a fast double windup, a slow quadruple windup. He threw overhand, sidearm, underhand, crossfire. Incredibly, most of his pitches, no matter where they came from, entered or just missed the strike zone.

His managers suspected that he would often throw three straight balls just to put the pressure on himself and add excitement to his pitching. Then he would throw three straight strikes.

"The best way out of tight spots is to fan the batter," said Paige.

He once walked a New York Yankee batter in order to face Joe DiMaggio. The mighty Joe D. had batted against Paige in a 1937 exhibition game on the West Coast and said then that Satch was the best he ever faced. Eleven years later DiMaggio still couldn't do much with Paige's pitches.

Satchel's stamina and his availability for work were legendary. He pitched in more than 100 games a year for 17 years. In 1934 he was in 30 games in 30 days.

"And when I say I pitched thirty days running I mean with somethin' on the ball, not just droppin' it in there," Paige insisted.

His physique was unimpressive and his energy

Satchel Paige pitching for the Miami Marlins.

was limited to purely selfish movements. His ambition was restricted to single-minded ideas of success.

"I loved baseball, but only if I won. Same with anything—cards, trapshooting, anything."

He won fifty, sixty, seventy games a year in every small town and big city in the country. His fame magnetized packed stands from Lost Woman, North Dakota, to Cleveland, Ohio. Wherever he went he carried a jar of snake-bite oil given him by the Sioux Indians. "Best liniment ever made for a pitcher's arm."

Paige's physical condition was naturally of vital concern to a man who pitched all year long for twenty-six years. At a height of six feet, three-and-a-half inches, and a weight of 180 pounds, he stood tall, spindle-legged, and lean-shanked. His stomach ached continually, the result of irregular meals in ten thousand dining rooms. His stomach miseries were the source of his famous dietary advice to pitchers: "Avoid fried meats which angry up the blood."

Paige's stoop-shouldered shuffle to the mound was a constant reminder of his oversized feet. He wore a size 14 shoe and, during his windup, would raise it high, shove it at the batter, and dare him to find the ball hidden behind the spiked sole. Paige's foot-in-the-face delivery aggravated all the other problems that opposing batters had to solve.

When he first started playing baseball—at the age of 10 in Mobile—Paige had two pitches: "hard" and "harder." Even then he shuffled along rather than ran. For, as he put it:

"You gotta go slow to go far. Avoid running at all times."

His gangling body, with big hands and feet flapping from his limbs, earned a boyhood comment: "You look like a walkin' satchel tree!" Nobody called him LeRoy.

Paige had a positive outlook on pitching.

"You got to know how you want to get the batter out. And then be able to do it. When you know where the ball's goin', you can do a lot no one else can. Out-thinkin' batters is when you take chances."

In his early years he depended on a slow curve, frequently thrown on a 3–2 count, to upset the timing of batters who always had to set themselves for the Paige fast ball. After he was 40, he threw any of his many pitches no matter what the ball-strike count.

Satch feared no batter, dared anyone to hit him, and would bet on his pitching arm at the drop of a dollar. The toughest hitters for him to fool were the ones who stood flat-footed at the plate. The punch batters, the slap-and-runners, the banjo hit-

Paige on the mound for Cleveland in the 1948 World Series.

ters irritated Paige. Then he would crank up into weird contortions and cock his left foot high.

"You never saw Ol' Satch throw harder," was the comment that always followed such displays.

In 1934 Paige pitched for a ball club in Bismarck, North Dakota. They won 104 out of 105 games against all sorts of opponents that summer.

Dizzy Dean led a team of major league all-stars in an exhibition series against Paige after the season. The final game, played at Hollywood Park in sunny California, has been dubbed "the greatest game I ever saw" by Bill Veeck.

The Dean-Paige duel lasted 13 innings, with Paige the winner, 1–0. After the game Dean, who was slick and quick and the best pitcher in the major leagues that season, said:

"You're a better pitcher than I ever hope to be, Satch. My fast ball looks like a change-up along-side yours."

Paige agreed. He was used to high praise.

Later, Dean said to sports writers, "Ol' Satch is my idea of the pitcher with the greatest stuff I ever saw."

When Paige heard these words of praise, he candidly admitted:

"That Diz is just about one of the smartest fellows I ever looked around for."

He may never enter Baseball's Hall of Fame, but Satchel Paige during his years of pitching earned his place with the best of all time.

CHAPTER **6**

Jay Hanna Dean

"DIZZY"

(Born 1911)

"Tell 'em I jest used to rear back and fog 'em in there!"

Dizzy Dean analyzed his pitching technique with that simple statement. A picturesque and garrulous ballplayer, he wasted few words on style. He preferred to talk about what he could do rather than how he would do it. He bragged about his ability, but he usually lived up to his promises. When Dizzy Dean said he was the best pitcher in baseball, he may have just been batting the breeze, but he was hitting close to the truth.

The 1930s were a time of depression, but Dean was on top of the world. No pitcher of his day commanded the attention or publicity that followed him and his career. His lively fast ball and zany antics were both the delight and the despair of his manager and teammates. His exploits were heroic and hilarious; he was both a great pitcher and a great clown. Had he not suffered an injury early in his career he might, truly, have become the greatest of them all.

To Dean pitching was fun; life was a game. He played to win . . . and to have a good time doing it.

"I never bothered about a batter's weakness. All I knowed was that he wasn't gonna hit any ball Ol' Diz throwed."

He had little concern for grammatical speech. He let his words flow freely with a natural rhythm and style. He let his fast ball go the same way, with a free and easy motion that gave no sign of extra effort. Dean was a big man who worked without strain. Like Walter Johnson he was both naturally fast and unnaturally sneaky. His "fog" ball was just a blur to the ordinary batter's eye. As Ray Hayworth, a veteran major league catcher, commented:

"Dean was the only pitcher I ever saw who

For four years in a row Dean led the National League in total strikeouts. It seemed as if he could throw strikes all day long.

could throw high pitches all day long and get away with it. His fast ball seemed to rise and sail at the same time."

It was obvious to professional critics that Dean had all of the necessary equipment to be an extraordinarily good pitcher. While he sometimes claimed that he didn't need a curve ball to get some batters out, he could throw a good one when he wanted to. And he could throw strikes all day long. He threw so many strikes that for four years in a row he led the National League in total strikeouts. In his 8-year career he fanned 1,154 batters, a ratio that would have put him among the all-time leaders had he finished out an ordinary great pitcher's full career. He once claimed that he pitched to a batter's strength because a great pitcher was supposed to strike them out the hard way.

Above all, though, Dizzy Dean was a showman, a sports writer's dream, a promoter's delight. His pitching was just a part of his personality, and he worked as hard off the field to promote himself as he did on the mound. Modesty is accepted as a positive trait of the ordinary great pitcher, but Dizzy Dean was not content to be just ordinarily great. He did it the hard way.

His pranks were childish at times but they were encouraged by the writers who followed him around. He would restage them for photographers, thus doubling his fun. His temper tantrums made headlines, but he never saw the need to apologize for being himself. He told the writers what they wanted to hear, or what he thought they wanted to hear. For years no one could pin him down to one specific birth date or birthplace. He would give out different stories and explain, later:

"Ah jest want all the boys to get a scoop!"

Dean was born in Arkansas, and his father claims that Dizzy and his brother, Paul, both learned how to pitch by throwing hickory nuts at squirrels. The Dean family were migrant workers who picked cotton for a living and therefore seldom lived high on the hog. Life was a hand-to-mouth proposition, and the biggest and strongest lived the best.

Dizzy Dean joined the Army when he was 16, and his first stint as a baseball pitcher came in San Antonio, Texas, near the base where he was stationed. The St. Louis Cardinals signed him to a minor league contract in 1930, but he was obviously too good for anything but the big leagues. In one season at Houston, in the Texas League, he tore up all the league records. Although the Cardinals expressed doubt that his off-the-field behavior was in the correct major league tradition, they put him into a Cardinal uniform in 1932. He won eighteen games as a rookie, and within a year, he was both the ace of the pitching staff and a trial to his manager, Frank Frisch.

In a clubhouse meeting before one game, Frisch was outlining the proper way to pitch to the lineup of the Brooklyn Dodgers, their opponents for the day. Dean listened for a while, making comments on Frisch's strategy. Dean was scheduled to pitch the game, and he seldom paid attention to anyone else's ideas about the art of pitching. Finally Dean held up his hand and said:

"Listen, Frankie. I won twenty-six games for this team this year and it don't look right for no infielder to tell a star like me how to pitch."

As manager, Frisch had the right to more respect from his players, but he let the insult pass. Dizzy proceeded to shut out the Dodgers.

Most managers like to play the game their way, but when Dean was pitching, the game was played his way. He once told the Boston Braves that he wasn't going to throw a single curve ball to them all day—just fast balls. It seemed a silly, and an impossible, challenge to a lineup of professional hitters. Dean was up to it. He shut the Braves out on three hits.

With his brother, Paul, Dizzy Dean dazzled National League hitters throughout the season of 1934. The Cardinals had a rugged and rowdy team that

The 1934 "Gashouse Gang": (left to right) Dizzy Dean, Leo Durocher, Ernie Orsatti, Bill DeLancey, Rip Collins, Joe Medwick, Frank Frisch, Jack Rothrock, Pepper Martin.

year. Frisch himself called them a gas house gang, for they often looked like semi-pros in dirty uniforms after a typical, hard-played, hard-sliding exhibition. With the Dean brothers, Pepper Martin, Leo Durocher, and "Ducky-Wucky" Medwick, the St. Louis Gas House Gang looked and acted like anything but a championship ball club. Their defense was ragged, and their hitting was spotty. Martin and Medwick used to look for hairpins on the ground before the game, claiming that a hairpin found was worth a base hit that same day.

But Frisch did have pitching. At least he had Dizzy Dean at the peak of his career. Diz won thirty games, the last pitcher to do so in the majors until 1968. Dean volunteered to pitch every day in September of 1934 so that St. Louis could win the pennant. The New York sports writers described him as superhuman during the last days of the season, and they were even more amazed when Dean pitched three games during the World Series, winning the first and seventh games.

Dizzy was also used as a pinch-runner in the fourth game. He was on first base when a ground ball was hit to the infield. Dizzy saw that a double play was a certainty, so he ran standing up into second base instead of sliding under the relay to first base. The thrown ball struck him right between the eyes, and he fell to the ground and lay motionless. His teammates rushed to his side and carried him off the field to the clubhouse. From the press box a writer noticed that Dizzy's brother, Paul, had leaned down toward the stricken player as if listening to something Dizzy was saying. Paul was asked later:

"What did Diz say?"

"Nuthin'. Jest talkin'."

Dizzy not only recovered from the crushing blow, with no more damage than an overnight headache, but he came back two days later to pitch again. Frisch was sincerely worried that Dean might not be in the best condition to work the final game, the championship game. When Dizzy came into the clubhouse in Detroit, Frisch asked him:

"How do you feel, Diz?"

"What do ya mean?" Dizzy said. "You want to win this game don't ya? Give me the ball and

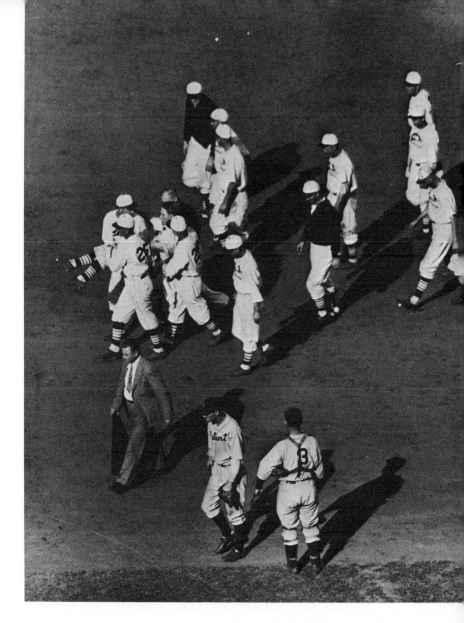

Dizzy Dean's teammates carry him off the field in the fourth game of the 1934 World Series. While filling in as a pinchrunner, he was struck between the eyes by the ball.

Dizzy (left) and his brother, Paul, dazzled National League hitters throughout the 1934 season.

your troubles are over."

Dean pitched a complete game, doubled, and scored the only run he needed. He was still feeling lively and coltish in the last of the ninth inning. By that time the Cardinals had an eleven-run lead, and Dizzy stood on the mound and laughed at the Tiger hitters. Frisch ran out from the dugout and yelled:

"Quit foolin' around or you're through!"

"Imagine!" said Dean later. "Score is 11–0, one out in the ninth, and he's gonna pull me!"

Reaching back for a little extra steam, Dizzy

threw a Dean special, "with smoke curlin' off it."
When asked if that was his greatest game, Dean
said:

"There ain't no use in me tryin' to talk about
any special game 'cause every time I had a ball in
my hand and that suit on, it was a great game."

Dizzy Dean pitched in four consecutive All-Star
games from 1934 to 1937. In his last appearance
he was struck on the big toe by a line drive hit
by Earl Averill, Cleveland outfielder. Dean limped
off the field to learn that his toe was broken and
that he would not be able to pitch for some time.
The Cardinals, however, needed him on the mound,
so he tried to take his turn before the toe fracture
had healed. Off balance because of having to alter
his stride toward the plate, Dean strained a muscle
in his right arm. His first sore arm was his last.
He never recovered from the injury. At least, his
fog ball was gone. All he had left was his reputation, his supreme confidence that he was a big
league pitcher, and his personality.

Not many pitchers could get by in the major
leagues with such equipment, but Dizzy Dean was
marked for greatness. In 1938 he proved it. The
Cardinals had sold him to Chicago's Cubs for
$185,000. He no longer could take a regular turn
on the mound, but when he got himself wound up,
he could still beat practically anybody. His record

of seven wins and one loss was better than that of any other pitcher the Cubs had, and his contribution to the Cubs' National League pennant was undisputed.

It was difficult for Dizzy Dean to become a great pitcher, because greatness demands a definite sense of responsibility. Dean wanted to make life and baseball a fun game. Pitching is work more than it is play. Dizzy Dean had the spirit of every boy who gets a kick from throwing baseballs. His route to success is not the best example for every pitcher, but he had more fun along the way.

"The only time you ever feel bad is when you gotta quit," Dean said soon after his career had ended. He had never grown tired of pitching, had never had the chance.

Frankie Frisch was asked one time just what pitcher he would like to see on the mound if the stakes in the game were a million dollars.

"With a million dollars at stake," said Frisch, "I'd pick Dizzy Dean to pitch the game. He loved the spotlight, but he was also the greatest competitor I ever saw."

Dizzy reaches back for "a little extra steam."

CHAPTER 7

Robert William Andrew Feller

"BOBBY"

(Born 1918)

When Bobby Feller was seventeen years old, he struck out seventeen batters in a major league ball game. It was September of 1936, and he was making his second start for the Cleveland Indians. Feller also walked nine batters, hit one, made a wild pitch, and allowed nine runners to steal bases. He recalls it as one of the sloppiest victories of his, or any other, pitcher's career. After the game his manager, Steve O'Neill, said to him:

"You had a good curve today, didn't you?"

From then on, and throughout his 21-year, major league career, Feller considered his curve ball his best pitch. Everybody else in baseball praised his fast ball. They said it was second only to Walter Johnson's. But although Feller's "fireball" may have been the most famous pitch of his time, it was only part of the technique of the great Cleveland right-hander.

Feller was a power pitcher. He could change speeds on his curve, and he even learned to throw a straight change up as early as 1937. But, as he said:

"I did my best by overpowering hitters."

His fast ball hopped, it sailed. It was once measured at 96.8 miles per hour. Batters quickly learned that young Feller was not positive about where the ball was going after it left his hand. He was, as they said, "pleasingly wild." Few of them dug in at the plate to face him.

The publicity that his pitching received during his first month in the big leagues was sensational. He drew crowds at every game he pitched—bigger crowds than any other pitcher of his time. Throughout his career his name was a box-office attraction second to none. Fans believed in the Feller fast ball. They thought that someday, in some game, he might just blow down every batter he faced.

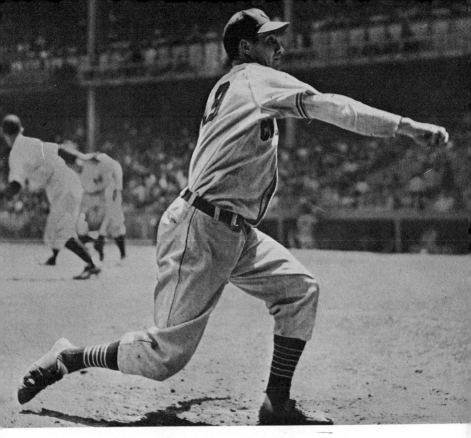

"Feller was a power pitcher."

From 1938 through 1941 he fanned 1,007 batters in 1,238 innings. The games he pitched were time-consuming. Batters didn't like to hit against him in the first place, and they didn't hit him very often anyway. He was strong and he could throw hard all day long. The fans who came to see him pitch always got their money's worth.

From the time he started his windup until the moment his pitch reached the plate, Feller was a picture of power in action. He dipped his body low, pumped his arms high above his head, lifted his left leg high, kicked toward third, swept forward in a long stride, and hurled the ball with full force at the catcher. The sound of a Feller fireball striking a catcher's mitt could be as loud as the noise of bat meeting ball. The fans loved to hear it, and Feller gave it to them as often as he could.

At the peak of his career, he was probably the best-conditioned pitcher in baseball. Although he was not a big man, he had a powerfully muscled body. He used every bit of this muscle to add momentum to his pitching delivery. Feller's fireball exploded, and his strong physique was what put the charge in it.

By the time he was sixteen, Bobby Feller could throw a baseball faster than anybody in the state of Iowa. His father was convinced that Bobby could be not only a big league pitcher but one of the best in history. When Cleveland's baseball scout, Cy Slapnicka, first saw Feller pitch, he too was quickly convinced. Feller was rushed to Cleveland, and soon the whole baseball world heard about his fast ball.

Feller wore a Cleveland uniform for the first time in an exhibition game against the St. Louis Cardinals. Frank Frisch was the St. Louis manager, and his Gas House Gang were the world's champions. Before the game Frisch, who was a playing manager, saw Feller warming up on the sidelines. He scratched his name from the starting lineup and said to the second-string second baseman, Stu Martin:

"Stu, you play second today. I'm not feeling well."

None of the Cardinals felt too good after Feller's first pitch. He was young, wild, and awkward on the mound. It was easy to understand that he might also be a little nervous; and no player wanted to get hurt in a mere exhibition game.

Feller showed little more than speed that day, but it was enough to fan eight batters in three innings. Within a month Cleveland's manager, Steve O'Neill, was confident that Feller, though far from being a polished big leaguer, could hurl the fear of the mighty into some big league teams. O'Neill started Feller against the St. Louis Browns in late August, and Feller fanned fifteen of them as Cleveland won easily.

Three weeks later Feller struck out seventeen of the Philadelphia Athletics. In doing so he set a new American League record, which he himself would break two years later. The game with the Athletics proved two things—Feller was going to be a great pitcher; Feller had a lot to learn. He

Carl Hubbell (left) with Bob Feller.

couldn't hold runners on base and he tipped off his curve ball before he threw it. Batters could tell by the way Feller held the ball that he was going to throw the curve, not the fast ball. They would then set themselves to wait until the pitch curved before they swung at it. Although he won five out of eight decisions in 1936, his first year with the Indians, Feller was just on the threshold of greatness. In a few short years he reached it.

The spring of 1937 was both encouraging and frustrating for the Van Meter, Iowa, farm boy. Feller impressed the New York Giants considerably in exhibition games. Carl Hubbell, Giant pitcher, said that Feller was almost as fast as anybody he had ever seen. Bobby fanned 37 men in 27 innings. Since the Giants were the defending National League champions, everyone in baseball was eager to see the young strikeout artist.

Feller started the second game of the season for Cleveland. In the first inning, on his very first pitch, he pulled a muscle in his right arm. The injury kept him on the bench until July 4, and there were times when Feller thought he might be finished as a pitcher. Without his fast ball he was lost.

Ten years later he was to suffer another arm injury. Pitching against the Athletics, he struck out nine of the first ten men he faced. With two strikes on the eleventh batter of the game, he threw a curve ball.

"I used to step two or three inches off to the left when I threw the curve," Feller recalled. "This time my foot landed on a pile of dirt, just a little pile of dirt. The curve broke over the plate and I got my tenth strikeout, but I also got a torn ligament in my knee and a knot in my shoulder."

The knot in his shoulder developed into a calcium deposit between the two upper ribs behind his shoulder blade.

"From then on, whenever I pitched, my shoulder used to lock. I never had a real good curve or a good fast ball again."

But by that time Feller had established himself as a pitcher. Not just a fireballer any more, Feller could be depended upon for nine full innings of smart pitching. Allie Reynolds, a pitcher who moved from the Indians to the Yankees, said:

"Feller didn't start to pitch till there were runners on base."

According to Feller, "The ability to pace yourself for nine innings is one of the most important parts of pitching. The great pitcher is one who holds a one-run lead over the last three innings."

In 1946 Feller won 26 games, starting 42 and finishing 36 of them.

Of course, by this time, Bobby was the mature, confident big leaguer that his father had predicted he would become. He was the most famous and the highest paid pitcher in baseball, but he earned both the headlines and the dollars he received. Great fame and a high salary can be a burden to a ballplayer. He must work extra hard and be extraordinarily successful. Feller's reputation as a strikeout king demanded that he establish the all-time strikeout record.

In 1946 he insisted on being in the starting lineup every fourth day and on relieving in between starts. On the 29th of September he fanned five Tigers in Detroit, breaking Rube Waddell's record for total strikeouts in a season. Eight years earlier he had fanned eighteen Tigers in one game, also a record. His pitching pattern required him to pour his pitches past batters and that's the way he did it. Pitching wasn't easy.

Feller won 266 games for Cleveland. Six times he was a twenty-game winner; eight times he was on the American League All-Star team. Some days he was practically unhittable. He pitched 3 no-hitters and 12 one-hitters during his career. The latter record may stand for all time.

Despite his achievements Feller must have felt at times that a frowning Fate was following him. His first arm injury, at the very outset of his career, was a meddlesome worry for at least two years. Although he was a winning pitcher in 1937 and 1938, he confided to a Cleveland newspaper writer that he thought his fast ball was gone. At the age of nineteen! The press greeted the news as a catastrophe and Feller was forced into putting on a fast ball exhibition just to prove to himself, as well as to fans and writers, that he might have been too hasty.

His recovery was quite successful. Between 1938 and 1941 Feller won 93 games. Then World War II interrupted his career and for three and a half seasons Feller was in the navy. After the war, however, Feller returned to the Indians a better pitcher than ever.

The 1946 season was Feller's best. He might have done even better the next year except for the shoulder injury that he later considered the turning point in his career. The Bobby Feller who had been a great pitcher with great stuff became Bobby Feller, a great pitcher with a lot of pride, determination, and extraordinary experience on the mound. It might be argued that Feller was an even better pitcher when he continued to win despite the loss of his fireball. Certainly he quickly developed a slider that was just as effective as any fast ball.

There are pitching coaches who say that the slider—a breaking ball that can be thrown almost as fast as an ordinary fast ball—will hurt a pitcher's arm. Others say that the slider more often than not will end up outside the ball park instead of in the catcher's mitt. Feller's slider should have convinced everyone that in the right man's hand it can be a great pitch. He controlled it better than he did his curve. For eight more seasons Feller pitched regularly and won consistently for the Indians.

Feller's long military service no doubt prevented him from reaching his goal of three hundred vic-

Joe DiMaggio hits a hard grounder off pitcher Bob Feller in a 1941 game between the Cleveland Indians and the New York Yankees.

tories. But he experienced an even keener disappointment in his pitching career. He never managed to win a game in a World Series. Johnny Sain of the Boston Braves beat him 1–0 in the opener of the 1948 Series. Then in the fifth game of the same series, he was hit hard and lost again. In 1954 Feller was willing and able but was not called upon to pitch against the Giants. The New York team whipped the Indians in four straight games.

Circumstances may have defeated Bobby Feller at times, but he won more often than he lost. He was voted into Baseball's Hall of Fame in 1963. A pitcher who could strike out practically everybody certainly deserved it.

Bob Feller grins from behind a big anniversary cake presented to him at a surprise party in Griffith Stadium, Washington, D.C., during July, 1956. The cake was in honor of his twenty years as a major leaguer.

CHAPTER 8

Salvatore Anthony Maglie

"THE BARBER"

(Born 1917)

There are two basic pitches: the fast ball, which has a natural spin; and the breaking ball, to which unnatural spin is added.

Fast balls are thrown at varying speeds. The natural spin of the ball off the pitcher's hand may cause the ball to sink a little, rise a little, or "sail" a little—left or right.

Breaking pitches curve. The arc of the curve may be big or little, flat or nearly vertical. It depends upon the force with which the pitcher throws the ball, the spin he puts on the ball, and the type of delivery he uses. The pitcher may throw curves directly overhand, side arm, or from somewhere in between. The faster he spins the ball, the better his curve.

Veteran catcher Hank Foiles once said:

"On a good curve the rotation is so rapid that the ball doesn't look as if it has any stitches."

A pitcher with strong fingers and a flexible wrist snaps his curve so that the ball looks like a spinning top as it comes to the plate.

"On a slider," Foiles added, "the spin is not so

Sal Maglie on the mound for the Dodgers in the 1956 Series. Although he won pitching honors in this Series, the Yankees finally defeated the Brooklyn team.

fast. You can see a spot on the ball about the size of a dime. Just as the ball gets to the plate that spot sails away from a straight line, maybe a couple inches or so."

The slider is the easiest breaking ball to learn and does not require wrist action. The slider is also easier to control, but it is not so effective as a good, sharp curve. Pitchers with *great* curve balls, however, are rare.

Sal Maglie threw curve balls; in fact he threw mostly curve balls.

Stan Musial first saw Maglie pitch in 1950. After the game he asked a New York Giant player:

"Where you been keepin' that guy? He's got the best curve ball I've ever seen!"

Musial's opinion of Maglie's pitching should be good enough for anyone interested in baseball. Although Stan The Man is known for saying nice things about everybody, he has always been candid about pitchers. Every major league batter studies pitchers carefully; great hitters know them perfectly.

Sal Maglie was 29 years old before he learned to throw a great curve ball. Previous to that he had pitched a very short time in the majors with the New York Giants, but he was considered just a competent moundsman. After his first good season, in 1945, he was invited to pitch in the Cuban

Winter League. Sal's record was so phenomenal in Cuba that the Pasquel brothers, who had organized a Mexican Baseball League, invited him to leave the Giants and pitch in Mexico. The Pasquels were spending millions to promote baseball south of the border.

The Giants had signed Maglie for $7500 but the Pasquels offered him twice that much. At the age of 29 Maglie figured he did not have too many years ahead of him in the majors. He thought he should get as much money for his pitching as he could.

Along with eight other players, Maglie "jumped" the Giants and headed south. Several players from other clubs—among them Max Lanier and Lou Klein, two headliners from the St. Louis Cardinals—also joined Mexican teams. Happy Chandler, then Commissioner of Baseball, banned them all from organized baseball for five years.

Money is important to professional baseball players and the Pasquels were throwing it around like jumping beans. But the standard of living in the Mexican Baseball League left something to be desired. Life was a series of long rides in old buses to spider-filled clubhouses and dilapidated ball parks. The American players had to eat strange food and they didn't like the taste of the water. "Gringo gripes" and stomach aches were common.

Sal Maglie didn't complain. And he did learn how to throw a curve ball.

"Dolf Luque taught me," said Maglie. "I was just a thrower till I met Dolf."

Luque, a Cuban, was manager of the Puebla team to which Maglie had reported in Mexico. He had had a long and creditable career in the major leagues, and had once pitched for the Giants. In later years Luque claimed that he learned *his* curve from the immortal Christy Mathewson.

"Mar-tee teach me," recalled Luque in his heavily accented English. "Mar-tee the greates' of all!"

Maglie was quick to discover that a pitcher's curve in the high Mexican altitude has to be extra sharp and perfectly controlled. Thin air reduces friction on the curve so that a pitcher has to add even more spin than normal to the ball. Sal taught himself to shave the edges of home plate, to drop the ball just on the outside corners.

With his new curve and increasingly fine control, Maglie won forty games in two years with the Puebla team. But by 1948 the Pasquels were running out of money and they cut the American players' salaries. Most of the men quit, returning to the States. But Maglie for one insisted:

"The Pasquels treated me fairly. They lived up to all their promises at first. I don't regret anything about the experience."

Three Americans who played semi-pro ball in Canada: Max Lanier (left), Sal Maglie, and Danny Gardella.

Maglie now had a great new pitch, but nowhere to use it. The major league ban was still on. None of the contract jumpers could play ball in the States, even in the minor leagues. For two years Maglie was in and out of a baseball uniform. He worked as a mechanic in a garage and pitched semi-pro ball in Canada while waiting for the ban to be lifted so he could rejoin the Giants. All he wanted was a chance to pitch. Maglie would have laughed if anyone had told him that he still had six big years ahead of him in the big leagues.

Born in Niagara Falls, New York, Salvatore An-

thony Maglie was a better basketball than baseball
player in high school. But he did pitch for a good
semi-pro team in Buffalo and once beat Satchel
Paige 1-0 in a game that led to his first professional contract.

Maglie spent two years with Buffalo in the International League, losing more often than not.
When he wasn't wild, he was bombarded by the
experienced pros. Finally he asked to be sent down
to a Class D league where he could learn how to
pitch.

Sal was not exceptionally fast, nor had he yet
developed any good breaking pitches. Learning to
move the ball around in the strike zone, to change
pace on his pitches, took time and patience just as
it does for any average pitcher. The lesser competition in the lower minors enabled him to sharpen
his control and his confidence. He won twenty
games in his final minor league season, but then
World War II interrupted his career.

After the war he won a place with the Giants,
who liked Maglie's looks. Mel Ott, his first big
league manager, said:

"Maglie won't overpower anybody but he knows
how to pitch."

Although Sal's technique was competent, he
needed an outstanding pitch to make it big in the
majors. Then Maglie bolted to Mexico, and there

Luque taught him the curve that Mathewson had given to him. It put Sal on the path to pitching greatness. When he finally returned to the major leagues in 1950, Maglie was ready to star.

Leo Durocher was running the Giants when Maglie reported to the team's spring training camp at Phoenix. While Maglie was pitching batting practice one day, Durocher stood behind the batting cage marveling at Sal's curve-ball control.

"Watch this guy," Leo said to Jim McCulley, writer for the New York *Daily News*. "He's just like a barber the way he shaves those corners."

McCulley nicknamed Sal, "The Barber," and Maglie lived up to the legend. Gaunt-faced and black-bearded, despite a daily razor, Maglie would brush a batter's chin with a fast ball, then clip the outside corner with his curve. The hitters paid the price for facing the Barber, and the Giants rang up profits.

In one memorable stretch of mid-summer pitching, Maglie was unscored on in forty-five consecutive innings. His pitching pattern was simple:

"I threw fast balls high and tight so the batter couldn't get set. When I came back with a curve low and away, he'd have to reach for it. That's the only way to pitch and win."

Frustrated National League batters moaned and groaned. They complained that his brushback

Adolfo Luque, who helped Maglie perfect his curve.

The camera catches a 1952 Maglie pitch.

pitches were beanballs. The Cincinnati Reds said
his curve was really a spit ball. The Dodgers, on
whom he was particularly rough, said he cut the
ball with his belt buckle or fingernail before he
threw it.

He is hurling against the Pirates.

On April 19, 1952, at Ebbets Field he shut out Brooklyn. It was the first time that had happened in 177 games. When asked how he pitched that day, Maglie said:

"What did I throw? Curves, mostly curves. What

"The Barber" pitches the first ball of the 1956 World Series to Hank Bauer.

Teammate Jackie Robinson (42) congratulates Sal Maglie for pitching a no-hitter.

else have I got?"

An admiring Warren Spahn said that Maglie "could curve a baseball into a milk bottle." What more could a pitcher want?

A college professor published a story in a national magazine that stated: "Nobody can make a baseball curve."

Maglie just frowned and said: "I'll take that guy, stand him behind a tree, and I'll break a pitch around that tree and hit him . . . or give him my month's salary check."

Twice Maglie pitched the Giants to the National League title. Durocher used him in the pennant-clinching game in both 1951 and 1954. Maglie was the money pitcher.

On the mound Maglie was a picture of powerfully intense concentration. Proper control of the curve ball is difficult even for a craftsman. The glare from beneath Maglie's black brows reflected his conviction that retiring any batter meant hard work.

Maglie's right leg was shorter than his left, a problem that was partly corrected by wearing a leather pad, three-eighths of an inch thick, under his right heel. Still, Sal's spine was constantly strained by the violent contortions to which he subjected it while in the act of throwing curve balls. His aching back eventually took most of the pleasure out of pitching.

In 1956 he was purchased by the Dodgers, a team that he had beaten twenty-three times while pitching for the Giants. Although Maglie was not finally released for two more years, the season of 1956 climaxed his career.

He won thirteen games for the pennant-winning Dodgers, pitched a no-hit game against Philadelphia on September 26, 1956, and beat the Yankees 6–3 in the World Series.

Every pitcher recalls with pleasure his no-hitter, the game that puts his name in the record book. Maglie smiles at the memory of the last out, an easy grounder hit off a good curve. Dodger second baseman, Jim Gilliam, scooped it up and threw the batter out as Maglie let out a happy cry.

But, just as irony touched much of Maglie's career, it also touched his second Series start that year. Although he pitched almost as well as he had in his no-hitter, the Yankees' Don Larsen pitched the only perfect game in World Series history, beating the Dodgers, 2-0.

"Not many people remember I was in that game," says Maglie, ruefully.

Master of the curve, Sal Maglie should have no fears.

He'll be remembered.

CHAPTER 9

Warren Edward Spahn

"THE HOOK"

(Born 1921)

In 1942 Casey Stengel first saw Warren Spahn throw a baseball. "That boy could be great," he said. Stengel's prophecy was concise and absolutely true. Warren Spahn was to become the best pitcher the Braves had ever had in their lineup—perhaps the finest left-hander of all time.

Spahn's pitching form struck Stengel as nearly perfect. And his delivery excited spectators—fans and professionals alike—for more than two decades. He wasted no motions. A picture-pitcher, he coördinated windup, kick, step, and throw into one continuously smooth operation.

Even the batter in the box could not help but admire Spahn's pitch. Hitting it was something else. Few batters did so consistently. When any batter indicated that he didn't mind—even liked—to hit against Spahn, Warren went to work. He toyed with a tough hitter, changed his pattern of pitching, improved his pitches, developed new ones, until that tough hitter was just another out-man.

"The more I pitched to a hitter the less I was impressed by him," said Spahn.

Hitters came to and disappeared from the baseball scene but Spahn pitched on, winning more games than any left-hander in history. Most baseball men thought Spahn's four years in the army (1940–1943) would prevent him from setting any all-time records. Few pitchers survive beyond the age of 35 in the daily battle to win ball games. Yet in 1962, at the age of 41, Spahn equaled the best record of his ever-successful career, winning 23 games and losing 7 for a sixth-place ball club.

Form, despite its perfection, does not frighten batters back to the bench. And Spahn's smooth motion made success look easy for a hitter. But his strong left hand and a supple, flexible wrist triggered a barrel-full of "live" baseballs. The path of his pitches was seldom straight. They wiggled, they

"Spahn toyed with a tough hitter."

sailed, they sank, they curved. Sometimes they looked faster than they were, for Spahn was one of the best at "pulling the string." He changed the speed of his pitch without changing his motion during the delivery.

Appearances can be deceiving in baseball. Spahn mastered deception. His brisk windup, effortless delivery, and neat follow-through looked too simple to be true.

"He looks so *easy* to hit," said Cincinnati outfielder Frank Robinson, with a puzzled frown. Robby seldom bothered Spahn.

"I can't figure him out," said Stan Musial, with a sly grin. But "Stan the Man," as shrewd as he was skillful, hit Spahn as if he owned him.

Unfortunately for baseball, fortunately for Spahn, there was just one Musial.

At the age of nine, skinny Spahn was a first baseman. He played for the Lake City Athletic Club in Buffalo, New York. His father not only encouraged him but actually played on the same team when Spahn reached his teens.

The South Park High School baseball team presented Warren with a problem. The school's first baseman was better than he was, so he went to the mound—a significant move on his part.

Spahn was left-handed, threw overhand, and was

faster than any pitcher in town. Schoolboy batters respected him, major league scouts doted on him. Both Boston clubs, the Red Sox and the old Braves, wanted him. The Red Sox lost when scout Billy Meyer persuaded Spahn to sign with Bradford, Pennsylvania, a Brave farm team.

In his first professional season Spahn hurt his arm, pulling tendons in his shoulder. For many pitchers that might have been a bad start. For Spahn it was, in a way, a good break. He learned a most important lesson. A professional pitcher's arm is the tool of his trade. Stiff, tired, worn at the edges, that arm must still do the job. He must take it to the mound and work with it.

Spahn was not a stoic or a throwback to the ancient Spartans, who were taught to ignore all pain. He had occasional brief periods of injury-caused inactivity during his career. But annually, from 1947 through 1963, his totaled work sheet in the major leagues showed a remarkable consistency. Many of his records stemmed from his dogged willingness to work. *Innings Pitched* is a drab statistic but Spahn's volume of effort (4,874 innings through 1963) is admired by fellow pros as much as his other records.

In his first seven seasons with the Braves, located at that time in Boston, Spahn was primarily a fast-ball pitcher. With his marvelous motion he

threw a straight change-of-pace. And occasionally he used a slow curve ball. Spahn claimed that he never had a *good* curve ball. He always wished for one, and he insisted that he would work until he came up with one. (In the spring of 1964, 43-year-old Spahn was still developing his curve.)

In 1952 Spahn suffered his first and only "poor" season. He won 14, lost 19. It was the first time since becoming a professional that he had lost more games than he won. As a result, he learned another lesson.

"I had to change my style, my pitching pattern," he said. "The hitters were telling me so." Spahn was irritated when batters connected with his pitches, but he quickly learned how to throw off their timing.

Spahn developed a screwball, a sinking pitch that batters beat into the ground more often than not. More tantalizing than sharp-breaking, Spahn's "scroogie" annoyed hitters. His carefully controlled motion gave no hint of the type of pitch he was delivering. Batters had to wait, watch for the spin and break of the screwball. Yet they had to be ready also for the fast ball, for Spahn was still

Lefty Warren Spahn throws the first ball in the second game of the 1948 World Series at Braves Field, Boston.

fast enough to get the ball by them.

With his steady, always consistent form Spahn exercised tight control on each of his deliveries. Most pitchers work for years just to be able to throw the ball consistently *into* the strike zone. Spahn worked *just on the edges,* or *just outside,* the strike zone.

"The plate is seventeen inches wide," he noted. "I try to avoid the foot in the middle. I pitch to the two-and-a-half inches on each side."

Spahn's formula for success sounded as effortless as his form on the mound looked. But mathematical precision is not so easy to maintain with the ever-changing human body. The aging Spahn spent most of his off-season days in quiet relaxation, resting for his annual seven-month baseball duty.

In Hartshorne, Oklahoma, his 800-acre cattle ranch provided just enough recreation to keep his legs loose, his weight down. He fished, he swam, he walked about wondering which young pitcher would try to take his job away the next spring. Young pitchers inspired him as much as he inspired them.

"They're all after my job. When they're good, I'm better. I have to be."

Spahn's unsmiling seriousness on the mound had an analytical, philosophical bent. He rarely raged at misfortune. Errors, bad pitches, lost ball games irri-

Spahn checks Yankee rival Whitey Ford's pitching arm. Both men were on the mound during the 1957 World Series.

tated him. Nevertheless he merely cocked his head to one side, distilled whatever knowledge he could from his own performance, and prepared for the next game. In his own way he was sportsmanlike. He learned how *not* to lose gracefully.

Off the mound Spahn was coltish—a smiler, a quipster. He was a playful prankster who liked his own jokes and wanted everyone else to do so. He laughed at himself, proud of the nose that earned him the nickname *"Hook."* He brushed his hair back and up, leaving a slope of bone that dropped to an attention-getting point. Forever a Brave, he looked the part of the Big Chief.

When he wasn't joking, though, Spahn talked about his trade. His constant comment on pitches, pitching, and pitchers was excellent counsel for young Brave pitchers. And by his own example he proved the worth of his good advice.

"Sometimes I get behind on batters deliberately," he has said. "Makes them hungry for fat pitches. I made a living on hungry hitters."

(Of course he seldom gave a hitter a fat pitch to hit.)

Confidence in his arm, concentration on his control, and consistency in his motion made Spahn a winner.

"When I'm on the mound I'm the very best pitcher in the league!" Spahn would insist, as all great pitchers do.

His managers knew that an assignment for Spahn to pitch the next day was a good reason for them to get a good night's sleep.

"Just go to bed and forget about him," said Charley Dressen, in 1961. "Spahn never walks anybody and you can't steal on him. What more does a pitcher want?"

Spahn wanted everything to be perfect. His move to first base was so good that base runners simply forgot about stealing second and concentrated on not getting picked off base. Spahn fielded his position like any good infielder. He hit more home runs than any other pitcher on record and ran the bases well enough to be used as a pinch runner.

"Anything you can do to help win a ball game makes you a better pitcher," he said with positive concern for buttering his own bread.

Through 1964 Spahn won 20 games in 13 different seasons. And that twentieth win always marked his best game of that particular season.

"Winning twenty games a year pays off in salary and reputation. Those things keep a player in business," he said.

Spahn also pitched two no-hitters, but he remembered especially his 300th major league victory on August 11, 1961. He said afterward:

"That was my biggest personal thrill. It was a good, low-scoring game (2–1). I was glad it was over. Just imagine. Three hundred wins! Walter Johnson, Christy Mathewson, and now me. It seems almost immoral."

A modest champion, Spahn deserved everything good that he got.

CHAPTER **10**

Edward Charles Ford

"WHITEY"

(Born 1928)

Whitey Ford has never been more than 5 feet, 10 inches tall. The typical major league baseball scout would say he's too short to be a great baseball pitcher. Pitching demands the strength and stamina of big men; long, strong legs to start the pitching motion; long, supple arms and wrists to sling the ball toward the plate.

Whitey Ford is stubby and stocky. But he's also clever and cocky. His fast ball has no more speed than the average big league fast ball, but as he puts it:

Ford puts his whole body to work on each pitch.

"It's fast enough and it moves. One time it sails a little bit, another time it sinks. Depends on how I throw it."

To Ford all good pitching depends upon where the ball is thrown.

"You try to put the ball where you want it to go . . . and where the batter doesn't want it." Essentially pitching, then, is easy.

Ford's self-confidence is a basic part of his pitching equipment. He knows himself; knows what he can do and what he can't do. That knowledge is more important to a pitcher than height and reach.

Here he is on the mound in the 1956 World Series.

Ford is blessed with excellent physical coördination and good balance. He wastes none of the effort he puts into pitching. In his smooth, deliberate motion he can put his whole body to work on each pitch. That requires more effort for him than for a big man with natural "stuff," but the results are similar. Control to a pitcher is simply a combination of mind and body working together.

"A pitcher," says Ford, "has to know what he has and what he doesn't have."

Ford throws two different types of fast balls, several curves, and a slider, and he varies the speed on all of them. To control each variation requires an extraordinary amount of concentration. Whitey on the mound is like a machine that clicks, whirs, and spins into action for each pitch.

Because he is a comparatively little man, his self-confidence is called cockiness; his attitude is considered brash and arrogant. But all pitchers, especially the great ones, must have a certain amount of conceit. To be extra good they must be extra confident in their abilities. If Ford were 6 feet tall and weighed 200 pounds, he would be called overpowering, even if he had just the same pitching equipment.

In developing his physical style, Ford's self-assurance was a distinct advantage. He was always willing to take advice on pitching, but he used that advice only when he thought it was of particular benefit to his talents. Not every pitcher can or will make that choice. Yet all pitchers are individuals with certain limitations. They grip the ball differently; they throw it from different angles; they release it in different ways. Ford concentrated on doing it his way. Trial and error, patience and practice enabled him to reduce pitching problems to his own personal solution.

George Weiss, when he was general manager of the New York Yankees, found Ford's attitude to be exasperating.

"He is a typical fresh New York kid who aggravates you out of sheer contrariness."

Ford frequently insisted on doing things his way but only when he was certain that his way was the best way. His record bears out the accuracy of his conviction. Ford has not only been a big winner for the Yankees; his won-lost percentage and earned-run average are among the best in baseball history.

Born in Manhattan on October 21, 1928, Edward Charles Ford liked baseball so much that, when he found out his high school didn't have a baseball team, he switched schools. As a teenager he was good enough to earn tryouts with both the Dodgers, then in Brooklyn, and the Yankees.

The Yankees signed him in September of 1946, and the Dodgers soon realized they had made a mistake by not grabbing him themselves.

"By July of '47 I knew we had goofed," said Fresco Thompson, the Dodgers' chief of player procurement. "Everybody looks for big kids who can really fog the baseball. Ford was small but he had courage and the curve of a pro with ten years' experience."

Ford spent four years in the Yankee farm system. When they brought him to the majors in 1950 the Yankees were, as usual, fighting for the

American League pennant. Ford was knocked out in his first appearance in the big leagues, but he then won six straight games and was considered the fourth starter on a staff that included Vic Raschi, Allie Reynolds, and Eddie Lopat.

In the final weeks of the season, when Detroit was battling the Yankees for first place, Ford whipped the Tigers 8–1. When asked if that was the biggest game he had ever pitched, he said:

"I remember beating Astoria 17–11 when I was pitching for Maspeth. That was a good one, too."

His reputation as a cocky young man was established, but by that time he knew that he could do a job in the majors. If a good pitcher was supposed to win ball games then he was a good pitcher; it didn't make much difference who the opposing club was.

During the 1951 and 1952 seasons Ford was in the Army at Ft. Devens, Massachusetts. He came back to the Yankees with what he called "half the stuff I used to have." American League batters couldn't tell the difference. He was a big winner for New York for four straight years, and his reputation as a craftsman grew each season. Casey Stengel called him "my little 'perfessor'," and the conviction grew that Ford had to be smart because he was small.

In his own mind Ford felt that his style was

Whitey Ford and Manager Casey Stengel (right) celebrate the Yanks' fourth straight victory over the Phils in the 1950 World Series.

successful not because of brains but because of control. He said:

"If a guy has a good fast ball, a good curve, and good control, he doesn't need brains. If he has a good fast ball, a good curve, and *no* control, no amount of brains can help him."

For years Ford was known as a curve-ball pitcher. He threw a sweeping sidearm curve and an overhand curve that dropped almost straight down. He changed speeds on both curves and was able to throw them no matter what the count on the batter. When batters looked for his curve, though, he could and did throw a pretty good fast ball. He tried to stay one step ahead of the batter if he could.

"Some batters never guess, never look for a certain type of pitch. But most of them do. Baseball is a guessing game, pitcher versus batter."

While he approached every pitch with confidence, Ford knew that baseball pitching is an imperfect art.

"You're bound to make mistakes during a game. I make maybe ten mistakes a game, ten bad pitches. Lots of times they don't hurt me. Sometimes you throw the ball right down the middle and even a good batter hits it into a double play. Then again, sometimes you make a perfect pitch, a curve down and away, and a guy golfs it into the stands for a home run."

In the long run the percentages favor the pitcher who knows the correct pitch to throw and where to throw it. A business associate of Ford's says that he has a "first-rate mathematical mind." Whitey collects information about batters from every conceivable source and uses that information to his own advantage. He knows that good hitters adapt themselves to the type of pitching they see during the season.

"What works one year, or in one series, won't work the next time because the batter is looking for it," he says. "So the pitcher has to adapt, too.

He can work a batter over the same way for a long time. But eventually the batter will catch up with him and then he has to find something new."

A good pitcher has to be stubborn, confident, and lucky. Good hitters will hit no matter how much information a pitcher can learn about them. But good hitters go into slumps, and a pitcher who works at his trade will try to find out just which pitch is bothering them. Ford trades information with pitchers on other clubs and files the knowledge away for future use.

"The best way to learn about pitching is to talk to other pitchers. They know."

The "book" on a batter is made up of opinions of the pitchers who face him in competition. Those opinions are useful only if they can be adapted to individual styles. A knuckle-ball pitcher's opinion would not help another pitcher who did not have a knuckle ball to throw. A left-handed pitcher's theories might not be of much help to a right-hander.

In general batters are high-ball hitters, or they are low-ball hitters. They can hit the curve ball or they can't; they are fooled by changes of speed or they're not. The percentages favor the pitcher who knows these facts and who can then control his pitches well enough to make the batter swing at something else.

Ford is a low-ball pitcher who doesn't like to pitch high.

"A good hitter knows his weakness and he may wait for you to throw to it. If he is a good low-ball hitter, he may expect you to pitch him high. Sometimes you go to his strength. Surprise! You get away with it once or twice and you get him pressing. He doesn't know how you're going to pitch him. It makes your best pitch, *your* strength, even more effective."

Whitey Ford has been called the best pitcher, pound for pound, in baseball history. Bob Feller called him "the best money pitcher I ever saw." Between 1957 and 1961 Ford was not a big winner. He wasn't able to win twenty games in any one season until 1961. Casey Stengel was accused of not pitching Ford enough during the season. Stengel would save Ford to pitch against certain clubs. If Ford didn't win many games he did win the big ones. His World Series record is the best of all time.

Feller maintains that Ford's chances of being elected to the Hall of Fame were damaged by Stengel's handling. Yet Ford has won over two hundred games and may even win as many as Feller—266—before he quits pitching.

Feller further contends that Ford should have completed more games than he has. In 1961 when

Whitey won twenty-five games he had only eleven complete games. Still, winning is better than finishing, and Ford says:

"I don't believe in pacing myself. I work as hard as I can as long as I can."

While he likes to joke and kid around off the field, Ford's easygoing nature changes when he pitches.

"On days when I work it's me against the other team. There's nothing funny in that."

When Ralph Houk, Stengel's immediate successor as Yankee manager, analyzes Ford as a pitcher he sums up the qualities of great pitching with these words:

"Whitey has all the pitches and he can control them on any count. Confidence, natural ability, courage, and an old pro's temperament. Ford has them all."

The little man who couldn't play first base as a boy because he was too small made it big on the mound.

CHAPTER 11

Sanford Koufax

"SANDY"

(Born 1935)

The pitching star of the sixties is Sandy Koufax, a man who is reluctant to call himself "great." He is the only pitcher in baseball history to receive a unanimous vote as "Pitcher of the Year"; he holds the National League record for total strikeouts in one season; twice he has tied the major league record for strikeouts in one game. He has pitched two no-hit games, and he has won fifty-seven games in two and a half seasons. Everyone in baseball except Koufax calls Koufax "great." His modesty is refreshing but unreasonable.

"I make mistakes. Lots of them," says Koufax.

All pitchers make mistakes, even great pitchers. The great ones get away with them more often than other pitchers.

"Sandy is the intellectual type," according to Los Angeles Dodger coaches who have watched him develop. "He's always looking for perfection."

The desire to make himself a perfect pitcher has driven Koufax to the heights of stardom. He has set the highest standards for himself, but he has the pitching ability to reach them. If his technique on the mound is not so polished as he thinks it should be, it has become progressively better.

"Sandy is basically a power pitcher but he has learned to control his curve ball. He always had tremendous speed on his fast ball and in addition to that his fast ball has a tremendous 'rise' on it as it comes to the plate. It is very difficult for batters to level on his pitches."

That analysis of Koufax comes from Buzzie Bavasi, the Dodger general manager who has sometimes been impatient with the progress of the big left-hander. Bavasi has suggested that Koufax might prove better than he was in 1963. In that season Sandy won twenty-five games, two World Series games, and the Cy Young Memorial Award as the best pitcher in baseball.

*Sandy Koufax pitches to Yankee Mickey Mantle in the 1963
Series. In the first game Koufax set a new World Series
strikeout record by fanning fifteen batters.*

Leo Durocher, a Dodger coach, said: "Koufax wins with speed and power, but he may get clever yet. It took Warren Spahn about ten years to add cunning to his pitching."

Koufax spent six years with the Dodgers, in Brooklyn and Los Angeles, always exciting comment about how great he would become, but never quite living up to his promise. He was signed for a bonus of 14,000 dollars and had to sit on the bench for two years without getting much of a chance to learn how to pitch. His wildness, inexperience, and ignorance of the technique of pitching irritated Koufax more than it did the Dodgers. As Sandy put it:

"You can't learn to pitch in the dugout."

Watching other Dodger pitchers during the 1955 and 1956 seasons was of no help to Koufax. His extraordinary talent had never been fully tested on a pitching mound. In high school he had not even played baseball until his senior year, and then he was a first baseman. What little practical experience he had had come in college, where he convinced major league scouts in two games that his left arm had championship quality.

The New York Giants asked him to a tryout, but he was so wild while warming up that they never bothered to call him again. The Dodgers also warmed him up, on the sidelines at Brooklyn's Ebbetts Field. He signed with them and went to spring training in 1955. He soon learned that pitching was more than throwing a baseball.

"I didn't know anything about fielding my position," said Koufax. "I couldn't hold a runner on base. All I thought about was throwing as hard as I could. So I strained my arm."

In 1957 the Dodgers pitched him occasionally, and in 1958 he won eleven ball games. But each time he went to the mound he was pressing, impatient to win. He tried to strike out every batter, and both his coördination and timing were erratic.

"The worst mistake I made was to get mad whenever I walked a batter or made a bad pitch. I still do."

Self-control leads to pitch control and Koufax still had a way to go. The frustrations that bothered him on the mound were compounded by a feeling that he was considered unreliable by his manager. He was learning with each game, but he was pitched irregularly. Whenever he had a bad game, he sat on the bench for ten days before he was given another start.

In desperation he demanded that he be given a regular job or traded to another team. The Giants, who had passed him by in 1955, would have been happy to take him. Willie Mays said: "Wish they'd trade him to us. He's got a fast ball you can't see!

And his curve jumps a foot!"

On August 31, 1959, Koufax fanned eighteen Giants in one game to tie Bobby Feller's major league record. He repeated that feat against the Chicago Cubs three years later but by then he had won his fight to convince the Dodgers that he could control both himself and his pitches.

His temper occasionally exploded, more at himself than at anyone else. His curious self-criticism demanded that he be a little better than he was and sometimes the tension would build up inside him. In a critical spot he would throw the ball just where a batter liked it and *boom!* went his ball game.

With more and more experience, his pitching rhythm settled down. A catcher, Norm Sherry, suggested that he relax a bit on the mound and not try to throw quite so hard all the time. His fast ball was still overpowering; his curve ball still dropped right at the plate. Moreover his coördination and timing improved and he was more at ease before each pitch.

Koufax had always had a reputation for being brighter than the average pitcher. His improve-

Giant hurler Jack Sanford (33) swings and misses, making it strike three and the final out in the top of the ninth. The strikeout was the 18th for southpaw Sandy Koufax in the Giant-Dodger game on August 31, 1959.

ment on the mound was sometimes credited to the fact that he had become a smarter pitcher. Whitey Ford commented: "Koufax isn't any smarter than he ever was. He's got better control, that's all. He doesn't make as many mistakes as he did."

Koufax was partly convinced.

"I still need better control. Sharp pitchers like Ford can shoot for the outside corner of the plate. I'm lucky to hit the outside half!"

In 1961 Koufax won eighteen games and broke Christy Mathewson's National League record for strikeouts. The Dodgers failed to win the pennant, however, and Koufax claimed that he got little satisfaction from his new record.

"Records don't tell how good a pitcher is. Winning is more important than strikeouts."

By the middle of July, 1962, Koufax was not only a regular starter for the Dodgers, he was the best pitcher in the National League. The Los Angeles team was riding his strong left arm to the pennant when an unusual blood condition caused Koufax's left index finger to go numb. He was sidelined for the rest of the season, and doctors feared for a time that his finger might have to be amputated. His chances for stardom seemed remote.

An operation restored the circulation in his finger, and he reported to spring training in 1963 with renewed determination and a bit of scar tissue in the tip of his finger. His fast ball was just as swift as ever, and he found that he could now throw his curve with more and more confidence. In trying to avoid walks, a power pitcher sometimes lets up to get the ball over the plate. Koufax was now able to switch from one pitch to another without losing effectiveness. The combination of great fast ball and great curve was too much for National League batters.

Koufax no longer worried about throwing strikes. He even asked other pitchers how *they* were getting batters out.

"Pitchers can help pitchers," he said. "They keep a file on batters and can review that information while they're standing on the mound. They don't have to pitch till they decide what to do with the ball. The best pitch you can throw is the one the batter isn't expecting."

Whether they knew what to expect or not, batters couldn't do much with Koufax in 1963. He fanned 306 batters and pitched the Dodgers to the world's championship. The Dodgers did not have much of an offense. They scored 200 fewer runs that year than in 1962. But as Tris Speaker, a great hitter, said:

"Good pitching can carry a ball club, even a weak-hitting club, to a pennant. On the other hand, a good-hitting team would be lucky to get a

poor pitching staff out of the second division."

Since Koufax was seeking perfection in each game he pitched, the Dodgers' weak hitting didn't disturb him as much as it might have bothered other pitchers. At least he rationalized it better:

"I always go for a shutout," he said. "Then one run is all I need to win."

The best ball game is the low-score game when the pitcher is the most important man on the field. Koufax became more than willing to shoulder the responsibility as he worried less about mistakes.

"If a pitcher makes a mistake, a great hitter will hit it; a good hitter may or may not hit it; a poor hitter probably won't hit it."

There are not so many great hitters around that Koufax has to worry about them. He has set his sights on winning at least 200 games in the major leagues. By the end of the sixties he may have to raise the mark.

The desire to make himself a perfect pitcher has driven Koufax to the heights of stardom.

CHAPTER 12

A Great Pitcher's Technique

As boyhood amateurs, baseball players learn that the pitcher is the most important person on the team. The biggest and/or the best boy athlete pitches. If he can't throw the ball over the plate or can't get it past the other boys, he is demoted to another position on the field.

"I want to pitch," says the typical boy ballplayer and that is a perfectly normal desire.

As boys become men, and Little Leaguers grow into big leaguers, the pitcher loses some of his importance. He is just part of a team. From an offensive angle he may be a liability rather than an asset. Few pitchers carry much weight with their bats. On defense the pitcher is the focal point of all strategy and what he decides to do with the ball affects the action of the catcher in front of him and the seven fielders behind him.

Great pitching dominates any baseball game. As Fred Hutchinson, a fine pitcher while he played and a fine manager afterward, said: "Great pitchers smother hitters."

The hardest-hitting lineup of All-Star batters can look like just another bunch of patsies against great pitching. When Carl Hubbell fanned Ruth, Gehrig, Foxx, Simmons, and Cronin in a row, he illustrated the powerful yet simple theory behind great pitching.

"We did what we planned and it worked out well," said Hubbell after the game. That is what pitching is all about.

The technique of great pitchers varies with the individual men who take to the mound. Different men have different approaches to the craft of pitching. Their skills are a result of study, of trial and error, of practice and concentration, of adaptation and adjustment.

Pitching is not an art, for a pitcher does not create anything new. Pitching is not a true science

because there is nothing to be discovered in baseball that hasn't been tried before. All the angles
have been explored . . . methods of gripping the
ball, of spinning the ball, of throwing the ball
through the limited area of the strike zone.

Great pitchers are not physical freaks. They are
constructed very much like the average man. They
are built no differently from the average pitcher.
There have been comparatively small great pitchers
but even the big great ones are no more than a
foot taller. Weight is relative to height and over-
developed muscles are a handicap rather than an
advantage.

Bobby Feller trained religiously. He favored daily
calisthenics and advised all pitchers to run, run,
run on days they were not working. On the other
hand Satchel Paige said:

"Keep the body juices flowing by jangling
around gently. Avoid running at all times."

All great pitchers have native intelligence, but a
high I.Q. has never been considered important for
pitching. Some pitchers are smarter than others,
but as Whitey Ford said:

"You don't need a Ph.D. to pitch."

The courage of a great pitcher is not measured
in terms of life or death. Pitching can be dangerous—Herb Score might have become a great
pitcher had he not been struck in the eye by a

line drive early in his career—but no major league pitcher has ever been killed on the mound. A pitcher must match his skill against the brute force of many batters, but if he loses nobody gets hurt.

Great pitchers are afflicted with proud conceit, but their cockiness and confidence is usually limited to the work they do on the mound. Warren Spahn can say: "When I'm on the mound, I'm the greatest pitcher in the league."

But Spahn doesn't carry his opinion off the field, and he is even willing to agree that Carl Hubbell was a pretty good pitcher, too.

The techniques of great pitchers don't lend themselves easily to comparison. A pitcher in 1910 had different problems—and different solutions— than a pitcher in 1960. Fast-ball pitchers approach hitters from different angles than curve-ball pitchers. Mathewson and Hubbell both threw a screwball, but Matty had two other good pitches and didn't have to depend upon the screwball as much as Hubbell. Each threw the right pitch at the right time and on that plane of comparison they were nearly equal. At that level all great pitchers are nearly equal.

If there is a common denominator among great pitchers, it is their ability to decide which is the best pitch to throw and to know that they can put it in just the right spot.

Two Cleveland Indians: Satchel Paige and Bob Feller.

Ford said: "You try to put the ball where you want it to go . . . and where the batter doesn't want it."

And Sal Maglie said: "I'd throw fast balls high and tight, then come back with the curve low and away, so the batter would have to reach for it. That's the only way to pitch and win."

A great pitcher is like a sophisticated machine. He is a combination of an intricate computer that can assemble information and reduce it to a simple direction, and an automatic weapon that can point at the vulnerable spot and hit it.

Sandy Koufax, who wants to be great and who admires the fine points of intense concentration, says:

"A sharp pitcher shoots for the outside corner of the plate."

Hitting that spot with a pitch that rises, sails, or sinks demands abnormal talent. Great pitchers do not throw baseballs on a straight line to the plate without giving an advantage to the batter. The spin on the ball as it leaves the pitcher's fingers can cause a special and peculiar rotation. The spin plus speed can give a pitched ball a certain, personal style.

Every pitcher must learn the best way for him to grip the ball and to throw it. To make his pitch effective he takes advantage of the seams on the ball, which can affect the spin of the ball as it flies toward the catcher. A comfortable angle of delivery helps his balance and coördination, and leaves his mind free for pure physical concentration when he pitches. Muscular strain is inevitable, but the great pitcher keeps it at a minimum.

Pitchers with great "natural" stuff—Dizzy Dean, Satchel Paige, Walter Johnson—were easy to analyze. Johnson threw a fast ball. If it didn't work he threw one faster. Dean would "rear back and fog it in there." Paige changed his grip on the ball and, by doing so, could make the ball jump, or slide, or sink on its way to the catcher.

The styles of the best baseball pitchers are highly personal. Some have to adapt themselves to circumstances. Hubbell and Maglie were blessed with no more than ordinary speed. But Maglie learned the perfect grip for an effective curve ball, and he concentrated on throwing that one pitch for strikes. He knew that the great curve ball is the most difficult pitch for batters to hit. Hubbell watched other pitchers "to learn why they were effective against hitters who were giving me trouble." Hubbell adjusted his delivery to develop an "unnatural" pitch, the screwball. It was tough on his arm; the strain eventually twisted his hand inside out. But the effectiveness of the pitch was worth it.

Bobby Feller was a power pitcher. "I did my best when I was overpowering hitters," he said. Constant exercise enabled him to maintain the leg, back, and arm muscles that supplied momentum for his pitches.

Warren Spahn was originally a power pitcher. But halfway through his career he had to adapt himself to a more clever technique. By changing the spin on his fast ball he developed a sinking pitch for right-handed batters.

A valuable Yankee hurler—Vic Raschi.

Allie Reynolds, another outstanding Yankee on the mound.

All great pitchers have control. Control is simply a matter of practice and concentration. Throwing the ball to the same spot over and over again may seem monotonous, but the development of good pitching control comes mostly with hard work. The great pitchers invariably are work horses. Their willingness to throw often reflects an understanding that practice makes perfect . . . or as close to perfect as possible.

Pitchers make mistakes in every game. The ball may not go where they want it to; the pitch they select may be just the one that the batter expects. But great pitchers make few mistakes, and they don't repeat them on successive pitches. A masterful technique that combines control, ability, and concentration will leave little room for error.

Index

(Page numbers in italics refer to photographs)